SNAKE POEMS

Camino del Sol

A Latina and Latino Literary Series

SNAKE POEMS

An Aztec Invocation

Special Edition

Francisco X. Alarcón

EDITED BY *Odilia Galván Rodríguez*

FOREWORD BY *Juan Felipe Herrera*

TRANSLATED BY *David Bowles* AND *Xánath Caraza*

THE UNIVERSITY OF
ARIZONA PRESS
TUCSON

The University of Arizona Press
www.uapress.arizona.edu

Special edition published 2019

ISBN-13: 978-0-8165-3843-0 (paper)

Cover design by Leigh McDonald
Cover art: *Francisco Mariposa* © Maya Gonzalez

Library of Congress Cataloging-in-Publication Data
Names: Alarcon, Francisco X., 1954–2016, author. | Galván Rodríguez, Odilia, editor. | Herrera, Juan
    Felipe, writer of foreword. | Bowles, David (David O.), translator. | Caraza, Xanath, translator.
Title: Snake poems : an Aztec invocation / Francisco X. Alarcon ; edited by Odilia Galván Rodríguez ;
    foreword by Juan Felipe Herrera ; translated by David Bowles and Xanath Caraza.
Other titles: Camino del sol.
Description: Special edition. | Tucson : The University of Arizona Press, 2019. | Series: Camino del
    sol : a Latina and Latino literary series | Originally published in 1992. | Includes bibliographical
    references. | English, Spanish, and Nahuatl.
Identifiers: LCCN 2018026894 | ISBN 9780816538430 (pbk. : alk. paper)
Subjects: LCSH: Aztec mythology—Poetry. | Ruiz de Alarcon, Hernando, active 17th century. |
    LCGFT: Poetry.
Classification: LCC PS3551.L22 S63 2019 | DDC 811/.54—dc23 LC record available at https://lccn.
    loc.gov/2018026894

Printed in the United States of America
♾ This paper meets the requirements of ANSI/NISO Z39.48-1992 (Permanence of Paper).

To all the Earth keepers!
¡A todos los guardianes de la Tierra!
Intechpa ixquichtin tlalpixqueh!

. . . ye no taamiqui
no titeocihui . . .
. . . now you're very thirsty
and also hungry . . .
. . . ahora tienen mucha sed
y también hambre . . .

Martín de Luna

CONTENTS

TAHUI

INCANTATIONS / SPELLS / INVOCATIONS

1. Penitents

2. Hunters

3. Farmers

4. Lovers

5. Diviners

6. Healers

NEW DAY

FOREWORD TO THE NEW EDITION
Life in Motion

Eight Moments—Francisco X. Alarcón, Liberator of Our Ancient Wisdom

1989—Loma Prieta Shaking Earth

Maybe it was the devastation from the 1989 Loma Prieta Peak 6.9-magnitude earthquake centered in the Santa Cruz area, where Francisco lived on Jesse Street at that time with his partner, Javier Pinzon—a temblor that shook the Monterey Bay region, uprooted the red and white-black roots of trees, disheveled mountains and sank Victorians in the Marina of San Francisco, toppled bridges in the East Bay, slammed and crashed automobiles, snapped the Oakland Bay Bridge, violently halted the World Series baseball game at Candlestick Park, and took sixty-three human bodies, extinguishing their lives and loves forever.

Twelve years after the 1977 first-year Chicano graduate student orientation at Stanford University where I met Francisco—twelve years of creative experimentation in the Bay, including literary organizing, international travel, teaching, dead ends and open vistas, rethinking and meditations on a new path—just maybe this grand earth-blast recast and rearranged Francisco's growing, new Mexica cultural self. All this new skin took form at the center of a performative poetry event, El Día de Los Muertos, that he and poet Juan Pablo Gutiérrez and a few others founded during the late eighties.

Mid-eighties: The Sacred Temple of the Mission District

Earlier, Francisco did something that had never been done. In the mid-eighties Francisco ambled across a quadrangle he had selected in the Mission District in the city by the Bay, bowing, lifting up, and igniting offerings of copal incense at every one of the four corners of the large square. He recited his Mexica Latinx poetry and chanted, "Tahui, tahui, tahui, tahui, hello, hello, hello, hellooo!" "Wake up!" he seemed to holler. At each corner an audience followed his soulful chants, expanding with his voice, shouting, and following his Street Shaman body in a multi-sensory, reverberating emancipation from a once-abandoned cultural space and place suffering a creeping wave of gentrification. Francisco Alarcón was intent on a Mexica "Aztec" poetics, a new self for all—*in open-air movement*—of deep healing and collective refiguring of the people's life-body. He wanted to reignite an ancient way of life and living—relevant, powerful, compassionate, and communal. Rather than resegregation, Alarcón envisioned *Totality*. Then—the

Loma Prieta earthquake. A few years later, in the early nineties, Francisco presented *Snake Poems* to the public.

Francisco X. Alarcón's Street Shaman Kit

This snake text, this new skin of our body, is at its heart a kind of Street Shaman's Tool Kit, what the Huichol of central Mexico (speakers of an Uto-Aztecan language branch) would call a *takwatsi*, a healing tool basket. It is not the usual compendium of poems or translations, or even a "total translation," as in Jerome Rothenberg's revolutionary anthology of the late sixties, *Technicians of the Sacred*. It is a translocura—the dream-visioned writing of a Chicano poet in full Mexica regalia with revelations of his own investigations regarding the last ethnographic materials forcefully taken and recorded by the Spanish colonial parish priest, Ruiz de Alarcón, in some ways, re-embodied by Francisco as he says in the work. This new snake material, if we attend to it, is also an act of *radical poetic liberation*—it seeks to not only to present ancient texts, once shelved in the Museo de Antropología Nacional in Mexico City. Its intention is more profound. Francisco wants to present the "poems" in this "Street Shaman Basket," in order for us to unlock many secrets and techniques of cultural snake power, a Snake Poetics—that is, the Mexica way of seeing, calling out, reconnecting, and sustaining a way of life that includes all beings, here and beyond.

The Colonial Priest, Ruiz de Alarcón—Snake-Talk

Remember, Ruiz de Alarcón's project, given his religious lens, was ultimately to deny the validity of the Mexica's Snake-Talk. Ruiz de Alarcón, I suspect, must have been pulled, in one form or another, by the profound presence of the Mexica, by their treatment of the spirit-world and its interconnections with all life. Without his notes, Francisco would not have carved a deeper text in a new time. A liberated version. Of course, here, we have to earn the Snake-Talk rituals, the essential teachings of the Snake Poems. To notice them, we must meander through these pages, read them out loud, listen to ourselves and the callings. Or like Francisco, we may have to demarcate four blocks of our neighborhood, wear Mexica regalia, offer our copal, bow to the Four Corners, and write our translocura and recite the Snake texts with the local communities. Snake Poetics, for Francisco X. Alarcon, I believe, is collective community return and re-creation of self.

Francisco too must have pondered much after he was shaken, and his home was tossed back and forth, as his streets and his Bay cities and as the oceans and mountains broke and crashed against each other as if they were calling for a new way of becoming whole again. He must have meditated on his role as a poet in the twenty-first century, on the question of Latinx writing in relationship with the vast, buried texts of Mexica Snake-Talk.

Late Seventies—Yoliliztli

In the Mission District of San Francisco, during the late seventies and early eighties, we all were shaken by the revolutions in Central America and their survivors of torn families slaughtered and "disappeared." We met the Salvadoreño and Central American poets, like Jorge Argueta, Cecilia Güidos, Roberto Vargas, Martivon Galindo, and many poets of witness at large—Alejandro Murguía, Jack Hirschman, Janice Mirikitani, Genny Lim and Tede Matthews and Philippe Bourgois, for example. They carried notes, images, journals and poems; they recorded the atrocities. Their voices were burning. Their hearts were mourning. Francisco wanted to heal them along with all of the city-dwellers, all of us, and the earth. Later, he would unearth a radical poetics of the sacred where our life, all life, continues in the task of opposing forces, in motion—yoliliztli—in true snake form, undulating freedom.

1978: Travel Fragment—Meeting Coyolxauhqui, Our Mexica Moon Goddess

We stare into the pit. Eleven years before Loma Prieta. We are at the center of a Mexico City that bustles with wanderers like us. We are dangling in its once hidden ancient Aztec Mexica center, Tenochtitlan.

We are at the edge of the main temple, El Templo Mayor, being dug out archaeological spoon by archaeological spatula. Two Chicanos from the Bay, a few feet from Coyolxauhqui (Bells-Her-Cheeks), thirteen feet wide and pushing herself out of the stone disk on which she is depicted. She is a moon goddess and sister of the patron war god of the Aztecs, Huitzilopochtli (Hummingbird-Left), who broke her body and killed her. Yet, she reveals herself to all and rises up from the centuries-old buried city once again. The Templo Mayor is split into four quadrants and is enveloped by serpents at its bottom edges. Eleven years later, Francisco Alarcón would make a similar gesture with *Snake Poems*.

Mexica Memorial

For this work and his many books, time, and love for the word of the people, let us honor Francisco X. Alarcón, the late poet, activist, and the people's cultural ambassador. A kind and compassionate gay man, a genius who gave all he could for us, who taught, studied, and traveled; who met many writers and communities throughout Latin America, Ireland, and Europe; who knew many languages and learned to speak and write in Nahuatl, who synthesized much of his work into one project by founding, with Juan Pablo Gutiérrez and others, El Día de Los Muertos, now one of the most popular cultural celebrations in the Mission District of San Francisco and throughout the United States. And let us thank Francisco for being the People's Philosopher, like other pioneers of Nahuatl thought and culture before him (among them Angel María Garibay-Kintana, Frida Kahlo, Miguel Leon-Portilla, Jorge Enciso, Alurista, Andrés Segura, Ysidro Macías, Tupak Enrique, Antonia Perez, Florencio Yescas, Renato Rosaldo, Jorge Klor de Alva, and Gloria Anzaldúa), for giving us long lost and abandoned ancestral concepts that we can envision and apply in one way or another, along with a Mexica performative cultural poetics that we have been attempting to build in the U.S.–Mexico borderlands since the Indigenista cultural revolution of the first half of the twentieth century. Let us thank Francisco—who died of stomach cancer in 2016—for this treasure of Snake Poems, which break many "impossible-to-cross" borders of language, symbols, Spirit-Talk, literary traditions, culture, and power; the ones that separate us from the first civilizations of the Western Hemisphere and, most of all, from our shaking-earth selves and our communities at large—all in spiral, snake-shaped motion—with the planet, its peoples, nature, and the cosmos.

My friend, Francisco. I will miss him, a luminous man. For many years to come.

The Way the Snake, Yoliliztli, Life in Motion—Twenty-Four Teachings from the Text

Here are a few of the many insights, revelations and findings that we can gather from Francisco's arduous project and study, this snake text. Perhaps it is more than a collection of verse—a way of life, unearthed from the once-captured and hidden roots of the Spirit-Talk of the ancient Mexica. It may be your time to step into the pilgrimage within the book and find your teachings.

1. The words of the ancients were assaulted, erased, changed, covered, denied—they can also be given life.
2. The ancient words are wanderers—from the South, from the North, from the Sun, from the Moon, from Mountains and Rivers.
3. As you recite and learn the words, you are bowing down to our Grandmothers.
4. You must know Cipactonal, First Woman, and Oxomoco, First Man—they are expanding points in the full spectrum of our bodies and lives.
5. Most of all these words have to do with intensifying "Spirit into Flesh"—that is, the "Plumed Serpent."
6. If you know the words you can begin to undo the mask that turned First Peoples into "Indians."
7. The words contain and emit the Snake-Talk of nature, of plants and the stars.
8. Recitation of the words provides the sound-maps to reach and touch the voices and beings of the First Peoples.

9. With these words, like tlamacazque, *the ancient priests*, we can keep the fire burning to achieve our transformation.
10. Words and incantations are ololiuhqui, *seeds of wisdom*, the harvesting of wisdom and healing.
11. Such words are ca ye niquiozaz, they serve to *cross time and space*.
12. Enter the mother, Chalchiucueye.
13. Seek and locate the ancestors, nichuicaz.
14. As Nahualocelotl, *the Wizard Jaguar*, you can chase away the oppressor, nican nihualla nicintotocaz.
15. Call the warriors, call them all—ca zan mochi nicnotza.
16. As the colonist approached, the ancients asked: What will take the place of our spirits?
17. Snake Poetry is Spirit-Talk.
18. Consider the *Snake Word Wheel* where all is one, ever-changing.
19. Words are eras, space(s), movements, solar cycles, tasks of and for ever-changing infinity.
20. We are nochalchiuhcontzinco, a *Jade Jar*, where the breath and cure of our growth and becoming are contained and charged with transformation.
21. We can serve as *turn-around potencies* and can reverse the order of things.
22. "*I, Spirit in Flesh*"—niTlacamacazqui, is the key to our being and the key to the way of poetry and words, that is, *Snake Poetics*.
23. Snake Poetics, the words of the ancient Mexica, once released by Alarcón's investigations and Street Shaman translocura can serve as *navigations into the "nature of Nature."*
24. Snake Poetics are part of measuring the divine, or the sacred in our lives, such that you can turn "caterpillars into butterflies" and achieve the realization of *life in motion*—yoliliztli, the *root concept of Snake Poetics*.

For a moment, with this rare and gifted book, let us wander with Francisco Alarcón's poetry-forces, let us burn the sacred copal, chant our collective voices of warrior peace and heal our split earth, sidewalks, communities and body. Let us raise a rising, singing collective figure of liberation in our communities facing deep challenges. Today, say "Tahui," say "Hello," to a new possibility of being, an ever-expanding Snake Poetics, as it may continue, in your hands—life in motion.

Juan Felipe Herrera
Poet Laureate of the United States, 2015–2017
February 28, 2018

BEFORE THESE POEMS, AND AFTER

This present collection is something much more than just another new volume by a contemporary poet. For as new as Snake Poems is, it is bound inextricably to the past. It is like the serpent of fire that opens up its mouth to meet its double at the center of the exterior ring of the Sun Stone commonly known as the Aztec calendar. This text by Californian poet Francisco X. Alarcón is an encounter with another test completed in 1629 by one Hernando Ruiz de Alarcón, a Catholic parish priest from Atenango, a small town in the present state of Guerrero, Mexico.

The poetry of *Snake Poems* emerges as an encounter with the Ruiz de Alarcón's colonial manuscript on Native American beliefs, *Tratado de las supersticiones y costumbres gentílicas que hoy viven entre los indios naturales desta Nueva España* (*Treatise on the Superstitions and Heathen Customs That Today Live Among the Indians Native to This New Spain*). Ruiz de Alarcón labored more than ten years compiling, translating, and interpreting the Nahuatl spells and invocations. The only extant copy of the hand-written *Tratado* is now found in the Museo Nacional de Antropología in Mexico City.

Ruiz de Alarcón's *Tratado* was compiled a hundred years after the Spanish conquest of Mexico and remains one of the most important sources on Native religion beliefs and medicine. Its importance lies in the spells, curing practices, and myths that were transcribed in the original Nahuatl, the language of the Aztecs. It is this language transcription that allows so much of the original speakers to come to us today, despite the compiler's insidious intent. Simply stated, Ruiz de Alarcón wrote on a mission for the Christian God, to expose heathen practice among the Indians and to extend the repressive practice of the Spanish Inquisition in Mexico. To gather the raw data for his catalog of practices, the author did not stop short of torturing his informants. Ruiz de Alarcón was admonished for his overzealous interview techniques and yet was able to finish his work undisturbed. Ironically, he was even promoted to ecclesiastical judge because of the extreme zeal of his faith.

Francisco X. Alarcón's poems reflect the worldview and belief systems of Indians of Mexico three and a half centuries ago. But clearly, *Snake Poems* is poetry, not ethnography, and the reflection it casts of the *Tratado* is nowhere near a mirror image. It is good that this is so. The poems are poems that stand as such, completely on their own. What Francisco X. Alarcón has captured from the *Tratado* in *Snake Poems* is the spirit of the Indian informants, a sense of Native culture alive, despite efforts to misread and suppress it.

Commentators on the *Tratado* frequently mention Ruiz de Alarcón's poor translation and weak evaluation of some spells in Nahuatl, which seem only guided by his religious prejudice and cultural bias. Francisco X. Alarcón reads *through* the *Tratado*, past the surface prepared for the Inquisition, down to the living speakers, whose spells and chants and beliefs are recorded, down to Martín de Luna, Mariana, Domingo Hernández, Magdalena Petronila Xochiquetzal, and other named Indians. And while their words can only come by way of Ruiz de Alarcón, *Snake Poems* reflects the gaps, the lacunae, the interstices of cultural survival.

All quotations and references that appear in *Snake Poems* come directly from Ruiz de Alarcón's *Tratado*, with five very telling exceptions. There is an invocation by the Mazatec María Sabina and a quote from the New Mexican weaver Agueda Martínez. There are allusions to living poets, to the Chicanos Tino Villanueva and Lucha Corpi and the Nicaraguan poet, priest, and former Sandinista Minister of Culture Ernesto Cardenal. For Francisco consciousness survives not only in the collective memory but also in the live words of the descendants of the original Indian authors. So, while the poem "Mestizo" celebrates the many strands that meet the hybridize in New World people, the epigraph by Agueda Martínez grounds identity very clearly, "ya que seamos hispanos, mexicanos; somos más indios": more than Hispanics or Mexicans, we are Indians.

There are 104 *Snake Poems*, not an arbitrary number but one chosen for its significance in Native thought. The Mesoamerican calendar is based on a fifty-two-year cycle: half of 104. It is as if one cycle was completed with the first translation of Nahuatl thought, Ruiz de Alarcón's *Tratado*, and the second cycle occurs now with *Snake Poems*. The first section of *Snake Poems*, "Tahui," contains twenty poems, one for each day of the Mesoamerican month. The final section, "New Day," contains six poems, alluding to the new era of the Sixth Sun.

The poems are spare in line length and in language. Nothing is wasted; very much is said. On the page, some of the poems appear long and lean like serpents on the desert floor. And there are the illustrations that somehow seem as much at home beside English and Spanish as they do beside Nahuatl. Beside the epigraph of Tino Villanueva's invocation to Tlacuilo, there is the image of the writer, the speaker, making words. Image and form intertwine with the voices and languages of the past and present: a poetics of ancient oral magic and modern verse. *Snake Poems* is alive with a simultaneously present and past passion and concern; it brims with the spirit of those who sang despite the fact that their very songs could lead to punishment and death.

Read these poems as expressions of life, as a celebration of the Native heritage of Mestizo America. Some poems uplift and some are humorous, and when taken together, they sing in collective spirit, vigorous, denying death. But then: stop reading, put your ear to the page, and hear the faint yet persistent echoes. I do.

Alfred Arteaga
English Department
University of California, Berkeley

ACKNOWLEDGMENTS

From Francisco X. Alarcón: Special thanks to Andrés Segura, tireless maestro of the Mexica-Tenochca tradition, the present and former members of El Centro Chicano/Latino de Escritores of the San Francisco Bay Area for their constant support and personal encouragement, and to the Rhythmagics of Santa Cruz, who have brought music and percussion to my life.

Poems in this collection have previously appeared in the following publications: *The Americas Review* ("Cutting Wood," "To Earthworms Before Fishing with a Hook," "Chicome-Coatl: Seven Snake," "For Planting Camotes," "To Undo the Sleep Spell"); *The Bloomsbury Review* ("Matriarch"); *City on a Hill* ("Traveler's Prayer"); *Five Fingers Review* ("Four Directions," "Hernando Ruiz de Alarcón"); *Guadalupe Review* ("Tonalamatl," "Little Toltecs," "Rainbow," "Canto a las tortillas," "To Cast Sleep," "Seer," "Reconciling"); *High Plains Literary Review* ("Herbs"); *New Chicano Writing* ("Silence"); *Puerto del Sol* ("Drought"); *Poetry USA* ("Against Unruly Ants," "Midnight Water Song," "Visions"); *Quarry West* ("Birds," "Domingo Hernández"); *Red Dirt* ("Against Anger," "Martín de Luna"); *Tonantzin* ("For Planting Corn"); *ZYZZYVA* ("Mestizo," "Ollin: Movement," "Ode to Tomatoes").

From Odilia Galván Rodríguez: A special thanks to Maestro Francisco X. Alarcón and Javier Pinzon for their trust in me to facilitate this project, to David Bowles and Xánath Caraza for their labor of love of taking on the updated translations included in this new edition, to Maestro Juan Felipe Herrera for his unwavering love and support and for writing this excellent and heartfelt forward, and to Maya Christina Gonzalez for her amazing artwork.

INTRODUCTION TO THE
SPECIAL EDITION
For Future Generations ~ Spirit Book

When Francisco X. Alarcón asked me to assist in making sure this beloved and cherished work was republished for its twenty-fifth anniversary I could not say no. He was about to leave us and go on that journey we all take alone. He had been resting quietly as I read to him from my most favorite of his books, which is this one. At one point, when I thought he may have drifted off to sleep, my voice got quieter and then his eyes flashed opened and he motioned for me to hand him the book. When I did he began chanting his own invocations and, as he did, more than spirits entered the room. I distinctly felt an opening to another place and time, one I suspect the Maestro had traveled to before. This book is another one of those doors he opened and invited us to enter. Here we get to visit a snapshot in time of an ancient place of Nahuatl-speaking ancestors. It is Francisco's poetic response to what he saw through their eyes and through those of Hernando Ruiz de Alarcón, whose colonizer's inquiry unknowingly preserved their stories, voices, and incantations that otherwise would have been forever lost to us. The everyday life of a people who were experiencing a great upheaval but were still compelled to share their way of life, rooted in the natural and spiritual world. This Tonalamatl, this spirit book, has inspired many to study the Nahuatl language and to seek out their indigeneity.

Francisco X. Alarcón is known mainly for his excellent writing, but I would also add his larger-than-life presence, his love of justice, and his always arms-wide-open approach to including and encouraging his fellow artists, whether they be emerging or established poets, writers, or storytellers. He loved all visionaries, the writers, musicians, visual artists, and activists—moreso I believe if they were also artists or understood how to include art in their movements. The group of talented writers I was lucky enough to assemble to assist in this project of bringing you this new edition of *Snake Poems: An Aztec Invocation* are phenomenal writers in their own right, as well as being educators and activists, something which they have in common with Francisco and me. We all felt right at home in this labor of love. As a comadre more than editor of this cherished collection of writing I am hoping that you will be as pleased as we are with the expanded translations and change in the book's size and format, giving it more of the feel of a codex.

Enjoy the journey that is this spirit book.

Ma xipactinemi—Be well,

Odilia Galván Rodríguez

Editor

AUTHOR'S NOTE

The only extant manuscript copy of Hernando Ruiz de Alarcón's *Tratado de las supersticiones y costumbres gentílicas que hoy viven entre los indios naturales desta Nueva España*, 1629, is in the library of the Museo Nacional de Antropología in Mexico City. This manuscript has a total of 109 folio pages and includes seventy-three different chapters divided among six main treatises. Not all of the Nahuatl spells in the *Tratado* appear in *Snake Poems*—only some of the most representative spells have been selected. The Spanish texts by Ruiz de Alarcón have been rendered according to the contemporary spelling of modern standard Spanish.

Diacritics have been omitted in the Nahuatl transcriptions, which generally follow the scholarly texts done by J. Richard Andrews and Ross Hassig (1984). The main departure from the work of these two fine linguists is my decision to follow the position taken by the late Mexican scholar Ángel María Garibay Kintana and align the spells as poems.

Many of the Nahuatl spells have several—sometimes differing—translations available in various European languages; these texts have been included in the bibliography. The parallel translations into English have taken into consideration all the previous translations into Spanish and English, but the author is solely responsible for any deficiency in this endeavor. The numerals provided before spells document the treatise and chapter where they originally appeared.

PRONUNCIATION OF THE NAHUATL SPELLS AND POEMS

There are only four vowels in Nahuatl (*a*, *e*, *i*, *o*,). The letter *u* represents the semi-vowel /w/. Nahuatl vowels resemble their equivalents in Spanish. Although long and short vowels have been recognized in Nahuatl, due to the inconsistencies in the *Tratado* regarding the use of diacritics marking the length of vowels, only a single value has been assigned to vowels in the spelling of the Nahuatl spells, as well as in the translations into Nahuatl done by David Bowles. For a more ample discussion on the pronunciation and standard spelling of Nahuatl, refer to Andrews and Hassig (1984).

Since the spelling of Nahuatl using the Roman alphabet was first introduced by Franciscan missionaries in the sixteenth century, Spanish orthography has served as a general guide for the transcription of Nahuatl sounds. Exceptions to this rule are the letter *x*, which is pronounced like *sh* in *ship*, and the digraphs *cu/uc*, pronounced /kw/ like the *qu* in *queen*. Though suppressed in the transcriptions of the *Tratado*, the letter *h* is used in Bowles's translations to represent the glottal stop, a sort of hitch in the throat at the end of some syllables. There are no diphthongs in Nahuatl. Two adjacent vowels correspond to two separate syllables. The digraphs (*ch*, *tl*, *tz*, *hu*, *uh*, *cu*, and *uc*) are considered single letters, therefore *atlan* is pronounced a-tlan; and *chiucnahui*, chiuc-na-hui. Two adjacent consonants are always divided: *axcan* and *calli* are pronounced ax-can and cal-li, respectively. Stress usually falls on the next-to-last syllable: AX-can, CAL-li.

SNAKE POEMS

Lo cierto es que las más o casi todas las adoraciones actuales o acciones idolátricas, que ahora hallamos, y a lo que podemos juzgar, son las mismas que acostumbraban sus antepasados, tienen su raíz y fundamento formal en tener ellos fe que las nubes son ángeles y dioses, capaces de adoración, y lo mismo juzgan a los vientos, por lo cual creen que en todas las partes de la tierra habitan como en las lomas, montes, valles y quebradas. Lo mismo creen de los ríos, lagunas y manantiales, pues a todo lo dicho ofrecen cera e incienso.

What is certain is that most or almost all present-day forms of worship or idol-atrous actions which we now come across (and from what we can judge, they are the same ones their ancestors customarily used) have their roots and formal basis in their belief that the clouds are angels and gods worthy of worship. They think the same of the winds since they believe these forces live everywhere, in the hills, mountains, valleys, and ravines. They believe the same of the rivers, lakes, and springs, since they offer wax and incense to all the above.

Hernando Ruiz de Alarcón, Treatise on the Superstitions and Heathen Customs That Today Live Among the Indians Native to This New Spain, 1629

TAHUI

Los flecheros llaman cuatro veces a los venados,
repitiendo cuatro veces esta palabra tahui,
que hoy no hay quien la entienda,
y luego gritan cuatro veces a semejanza de león.

The archers call four times to the deer,
repeating four times this word tahui,
which nobody understands today,
and then they cry out four times like a puma.

Ruiz de Alarcón (I:2)

Hello
Hola
Niltze

    tahui
    tahui
    tahui
    tahui

Four Directions
Cuatro direcciones
Nauhcampa

West	Oeste	**Cihuatlampa**
we are	*somos*	*nehhuantin*
salmons	*salmones*	*tatoyamimichtin*
looking for	*en busca de*	*tiquitemoah*
our womb	*nuestra matriz*	*toxillan*

North	Norte	**Mictlampa**
eagles	*águilas*	*ticuauhtin*
flying	*que en el pico*	*tipatlanih*
the Sun	*transportamos*	*in Tonatiuh*
in our beak	*al sol*	*notenco*

East	Este	**Tlapcopa**
coyotes	*coyotes*	*ticoyomeh*
calling	*que nos llamamos*	*titonotzah*
each other	*entre sí aullando*	*in metztli*
in the Moon	*a la luna*	*iihtic*

South	Sur	**Huitztlampa**
we turn	*serpientes*	*cocoah*
into snakes	*nos volvemos*	*titochihuah*
by eating	*comiendo*	*oquic ticcuah*
chile	*chile*	*in chilli*

Silence
Silencio
In cactimaniliztli

I smell	*huelo*	*niquihnecui*
silence	*silencio*	*in cactimaniliztli*
everywhere	*por dondequiera*	*nohuiyan*
clean	*aroman*	*in tlazolcuihcuililli*
nice homes	*las casas*	*cuacualli calli*
smell	*limpias*	*potoni*
banks	*los bancos*	*in tomincalli*
smell	*huelen*	*potoni*
so do malls	*y las plazas*	*auh in tiyanquiztli*
no deodorant	*ningún*	*ahtle popochtli*
odorizer	*desodorante*	*ahtle ihyacayotl*
or perfume	*o perfume*	*ahtle huelicayotl*
can put away	*pueden quitar*	*in quipohpoloz*
this stink	*esta peste*	*ipotoniliztli*
of silence	*del silencio*	*in cactimaniliztli*

Hernando Ruiz de Alarcón

(1587–1646)

eras tú	it was you	*ca tehhuatl*
al que buscabas	you were looking for	*in tiquitemoaya*
Hernando	Hernando	*tiHernando*
hurgando	searching	*tiquixtemoaya*
en los rincones	every house	*cecen*
de las casas	corner	*calnacazco*
semillas	for some	*cequi*
empolvadas	dusty seeds	*teuhyoh achtli*
de ololiuhqui	of ololiuhqui	*in ololiuhqui*
eras tú	it was you	*ca tehhautl*
al que engañabas	whom you tricked	*in tiquitentlamachiya*
y aprehendías	and apprehended	*in tiquimaltiya*
eras tú	it was you	*ca tehhuatl*
el que preguntaba	who both questioned	*in mitznahuallalaniya*
y respondía	and responded	*in mitztequihihtoaya*
dondequiera	everywhere	*nohuiyan*
mirabas moros	you saw Moors	*tiquimittaya in moros*
con trinchete	with long knives	*cuauhtic tecpatica*
y ante	and in front of	*auh itlan*
tanto dolor	so much sorrow	*miec chichinaquiztli*
tanta muerte	so much death	*miec miquiliztli*
un conquistador	you became	*otimochiuh*
conquistado	a conquered	*in pehualli*
fuiste	conqueror	*tepehuani*
sacerdote	priest	*in tlamacazqui*
soñador	dreamer	*in temiquini*
cruz parlante	speaking cross	*in tlahtoani cuauhnepanolli*

condenando	condemning	*in titecemixnahuatiya*
tu salvaste	you saved yourself	*otimomaquixtih*
al transcribir	by transcribing	*yehica tiquihcuiloh*
acaso	maybe	*ahzo zan*
sin saber	without knowing	*ahmo machiliztica*
el cielo	the heavens	*in ilhuicatl*
soy yo	I am	*nicah nehhuatl*
el de tu cepa	from your tree	*ipal mocuauhyo*
el de tu sueño	from your dream	*ipal motemic*
este cenzontle	this cenzontle bird	*inin centzontlahtoleh*
de monte:	in the wilderness:	*nemiuhyanco:*
tu mañana	your tomorrow	*momztla*

Same
Lo mismo
Tinehneuhqueh

we see	*vemos*	*tittah timatih*
feel taste	*sentimos degustamos*	*titlayehyecoah*
are so	*somos tan*	*tiuhqueh*
differently	*diferentemente*	*tinehneuhqueh*
the same	*lo mismo*	*yecentetl*

In the Middle of the Night
En medio de la noche
Ticatla

sobs	*unos sollozos*	*techocaliz*
woke me	*me despertaron*	*onechixtih*
I got up	*me levanté*	*oninococheuh*
and saw	*y me vi*	*auh ononnotta*
myself	*a mí mismo*	*nehhuatl nixcoyan*
in a corner	*en un rincón*	*xomolco*
crying	*llorando*	*nichocaya*

I'm Not Really Crying
En verdad no estoy llorando
Ahmo huel nichoca

it's just	*es solo*	*ca zan*
the sheer	*la grande*	*cencah*
number	*cantidad*	*miec*
of chopped	*de cebollas*	*coyoacxoyatl*
onions	*picaditas*	*tlacocotontli*
in the world	*en el mundo*	*in tlalticpac*

Shame
Vergüenza
Nopinahuiz

I washed	*me lavé*	*nehhuatl*
my arms	*mis brazos*	*oninopac*
scrubbed	*me tallé*	*oninomatequih*
my face	*la cara*	*oninixamih*
powdered	*jabón*	*in nahmol*
soap	*en polvo*	*alactic*
fell from	*cayó de*	*omalauh*
my hands	*mis manos*	*nomacpa*
but	*pero*	*auh*
my skin	*mi piel*	*in nehuayo*
only got	*se puso*	*zan*
redder	*más roja*	*ochichiliuh*
I was	*yo era*	*onicatca*
just	*sólo*	*zan*
another	*otro*	*cequi*
itching	*niño*	*cococ*
brown	*marrón*	*camilectic*
boy	*con comezón*	*piltontli*
getting	*alistándose*	*in ninomaniya*
ready	*para*	*ninocalaquiya*
for school	*la escuela*	*in calmecac*

Mestizo
Mestizo
Otomitl

my name	*mi nombre*	*ca ahmo*
is not	*no es*	*notoca*
Francisco	*Francisco*	*Francisco*
there is	*hay*	*ca*
an Arab	*un árabe*	*cen arabe*
within me	*dentro de mí*	*notech*
who prays	*que ora*	*in moteotia*
three times	*tres veces*	*expa*
each day	*al día*	*cecemilhuitl*
behind	*detrás*	*icampa*
my Roman	*de mi nariz*	*in romano*
nose	*romana*	*noyac*
there is	*hay*	*ca*
a Phoenician	*un fenicio*	*cen fenicio*
smiling	*que sonríe*	*in ixhuetzca*
my eyes	*mis ojos*	*in nix*
still see	*aún ven*	*oc quitta*
Sevilla	*Sevilla*	*Sevilla*
but	*pero*	*auh*
my mouth	*mi boca*	*ca olmecatl*
is Olmec	*es olmeca*	*in noten*
my dark	*mis manos*	*ca toltecatl*
hands	*oscuras*	*in cuappachtli*
are Toltec	*toltecas*	*noma*
my cheekbones	*mis pómulos*	*ca chichimecatl*
fierce	*feroces*	*yollohcocoleh*
Chichimec	*chichimecas*	*in nixteliuhca*
my feet	*mis pies*	*in nocxi*
recognize	*no reconocen*	*ahmo quixihmati*
no border	*frontera*	*ce altepenahuac*
no rule	*ni regla*	*ce tlatecpanaliztli*
no code	*ni código*	*ce nenayotl*
no lord	*ni señoríos*	*ce tlahtoani*
for this	*para este*	*ipan inin*
wanderer's	*corazón*	*yollotl*
heart	*merodeador*	*nenqui*

Matriarch
Matriarca
Cihuatlahtoani

my dark	*mi abuela*	*in cuappachtli*
grandmother	*morena*	*nocih*
would brush	*su largo pelo*	*quimopehpetlaya*
her long hair	*cepillaba*	*in huitlatztic itzon*
seated out	*sentada afuera*	*in oc motlaliaya*
on her patio	*en su patio*	*tlapanco*
even ferns	*hasta los helechos*	*auh ye in ocopetlatl*
would bow	*se doblaban*	*mocxicoloaya ixpan*
to her splendor	*ante su esplendor*	*ipepetlaquiliztli*
and her power	*y su poder*	*ihuan ipetl*

Rescue
Rescate
Maquixtilo

at the end	*al final*	*tlatzaccan*
I found	*me hallé*	*nehhuatl*
myself	*yo mismo*	*ononnottac*
holding	*sosteniendo*	*niquimotzoloaya*
the other end	*el otro cabo*	*in iyacac*
of the rope	*de la soga*	*mecatl*

Spirit Book

Libro de espíritus
Tonalamatl

pages	*susurran*	*in amaahaztli*
whisper	*suspiran*	*popoloca*
sigh	*cantan*	*elcihcihui*
sing	*páginas*	*cuica*
glyphs	*de izquierda*	*in machiyotl*
dance	*a derecha*	*mihtotia*
left	*danzan*	*iopochco*
to right	*glifos*	*imayeccampa*
I follow	*yo sigo*	*niquicxitotoca*
the drums	*los tambores*	*in huehuetl*
the scent	*el incienso*	*in ihyacayotl*
the stairs	*las escalinatas*	*in ehcahuaztli*
mountain	*una brisa*	*in tepepan*
mist	*del monte*	*ayahuitl*
sprays	*me rocia*	*quitzicuinia*
my hair	*el pelo*	*in notzon*
I learn	*aprendo*	*nicnomachtia*
to undo	*a deshacer*	*in xitiniliztli*
what is	*lo que está*	*in ye*
done	*ya hecho*	*chihchiuhtoc*
an ancient	*un jaguar*	*in ye huehcauh*
jaguar	*milenario*	*ocelotl*
roars at	*me ruge*	*hualchoca*
my face	*en la cara*	*ipan noxayac*
I start	*comienzo*	*nipehua*
singing	*a cantar*	*in niquehua*
all kinds	*todo tipo*	*nepepan*
of flowers	*de flores*	*xochitl*

Songs
Cantos
Cuicatl

> *xochitl*
> *flower*
> *flor*

Spirit Animal
Nahual
Nonahual

this whale	*esta ballena*	*inin hueyimichin*
can't stop	*que no deja*	*ahhuel*
singing	*de cantar*	*pinahuizcahua*
from	*desde*	*in icuica*
the bottom	*el fondo*	*hueyi*
of the sea	*del mar*	*ahuehcatlan*

Movement
Movimiento
Ollin

I call myself	me doy el nombre	ninotzalo
waterfall	de salto de agua	atl itemohuayan
Quetzalcoatl	Quetzalcoatl	Quetzalcoatl
spirit and flesh	espíritu y carne	inacayo iyolloh
Xolotl	Xolotl	Xolotl
his twin	su gemelo	icoauh
Oxomoco	Oxomoco	Oxomoco
the first man	el primer hombre	achtopa tlacatl
Cipactonal	Cipactonal	Cipactonal
the first woman	la primera mujer	achtopa cihuatl
the couple Tlaloc	la pareja Tlaloc	in namiquehqueh Tlaloc
and Xochiquetzal	y Xochiquetzal	ihuan Xochiquetzal
Centeotl, their kid	Centeotl, su niño	Centeotl, inpiltzin
and popcorn . . .	y palomitas de maíz . . .	auh immomochicintli . . .
I go on calling	me sigo dando	nicnanaltzatinemi
names	nombres	in tetoca
keep hearing	y sigo escuchando	niccemana niccaquiz
my mirror	a mi espejo	in notezcauh

To Those Who Have Lost Everything
Para aquellos que han perdido todo
Itechpa in aquihqueh oquipolohcah mocheh

crossed	*muchos desiertos*	*oquipetlatiyaheh*
in despair	*llenos de esperanza*	*nentlamatqueh*
many deserts	*son cruzados*	*miec nemiuhyanyotl*
full of hope	*en desesperación*	*netemachiliztica*
carrying	*llevan*	*quizacayah*
their empty	*sus puños vacíos*	*in cactihcac*
fists of sorrow	*de melancolía*	*intlaocolmapich*
everywhere	*a todos lados*	*nohuiyan*
mouthing	*mordisqueando*	*quicamapachoayah*
a bitter night	*una amarga noche*	*cequi chichic yohualli*
of shovels	*de palas*	*huitica iuhqui*
and nails	*y clavos*	*tepozmitica*
"you're nothing	*"no son nada*	*"amahtletih*
you're shit	*son mierda*	*ancuitlatl*
your home's	*su hogar está*	*amochan*
nowhere":	*en ninguna parte":*	*ahcan mani":*
mountains	*las montañas*	*in tepemeh*
will speak	*hablarán*	*moca*
for you	*por ti*	*tlahtozqueh*
rain	*la lluvia*	*in quiyahuitl*
will flesh	*traerá carne a*	*quixipehuaz*
your bones	*tus huesos*	*in momiyo*
green again	*el verde una vez más*	*oc ceppa xiuhcaltih*
among ashes	*entre cenizas*	*inepantla in nextli*
after a long fire	*después de que un largo fuego*	*in o iuh oceuh in tletl*
started in	*comenzó en*	*in motlatih ipan*
a fantasy island	*una isla de fantasía*	*tlachihchiuhtli tlalhuactli*
some time ago	*hace tiempo*	*ye huehcauh*
turning	*al convertir*	*in chaneh*
Natives	*a los nativos*	*chihualo*
into aliens	*en extranjeros*	*huehcachaneh*

Never Alone
Nunca solos
Ayic toceltin

always	*siempre*	*cemihcac*
this caressing	*este Viento*	*inin tenahuatequini*
Wind	*acariciador*	*ehecatl*
this Earth	*esta Tierra*	*inin tlalli*
whispering	*que nos susurra*	*in popoloca*
to our feet	*a nuestros pies*	*itzintlan toxci*
this boundless	*este anhelo*	*inin ayhuianyoh*
desire	*desmesurado*	*tlaelehuiliztli*
of being	*de ser*	*in titochihuah*
grass	*pasto*	*in zacatl*
tree	*árbol*	*in cuahuitl*
corazón	*heart*	*in yollotl*

Heart
Corazón
Teyolloh

fragrant	*fragante*	*ahahhuiyac*
flower	*flor*	*xochitl*
open at	*que abre a*	*cueponi*
midnight	*medianoche*	*tlahcoyohuac*

Dream-Flower
Flor-de-sueños
Temicxoch

in my dreams	*en mis sueños*	*itech notemic*
I smell	*huelo*	*niquihnecui*
the roots	*las raíces*	*itlanelhuatl*
of this flower	*de esta flor*	*inin xochitl*

I Myself
Yo mismo
Nonohmatcah nehhuatl

I myself:	*yo mismo:*	*nonohmatcah nehhuatl:*
the mountain	*la montaña*	*nitepetl*
the ocean	*el océano*	*niteoatl*
the breeze	*la brisa*	*nehecatl*
the flame	*la flama*	*nitlemiyahuatl*
the thorn	*la espina*	*nihuitztli*
the serpent	*la serpiente*	*nicoatl*
the feather	*la pluma*	*nihhuitl*
the Moon	*la luna*	*nimetztli*
the Sun	*el sol*	*nitonatiuh*
the sister	*la hermana*	*nitecihuahihni*
the brother	*el hermano*	*niteiccauh*
the mother	*la madre*	*nitenan*
the father	*el padre*	*nitetah*
the other	*el otro*	*nichontalli*
the ground	*la tierra*	*nitlalli*
the seed	*la semilla*	*nixinachtli*
the chant	*el canto*	*nicuicatl*
the cloud	*la nube*	*nimixtli*
the flower	*la flor*	*nixochitl*
the deer	*el venado*	*nimazatl*
the hunter	*el cazador*	*nimazamictiani*
the arrow	*la flecha*	*nimitl*
the neck	*el cuello*	*niquech*
the blood	*la sangre*	*nezzo*
the dead	*la muerte*	*nimicqui*
the dancing	*la danza*	*nihtotiliztli*
the house	*la casa*	*nicalli*
the quake	*el temblor*	*nitlaloliniliztli*
the lizard	*la lagartija*	*nicuetzpalin*

the island	*la isla*	*nitlalhuactli*
the shell	*la concha*	*nipachatli*
the collar	*el cuello de la camisa*	*nicozcatl*
the star	*la estrella*	*nicitlalin*
the lover	*el amante*	*nitemecauh*
the search	*la búsqueda*	*nitlatemoliztli*
the face	*el rostro*	*niteix*
the dream	*el sueño*	*nitetemic*
the heart	*el corazón*	*niteyollo*
the voice	*la voz*	*notozqui*
nomatca nehuatl!	*¡nomatca nehuatl!*	*nonohmatcah nehhuatl!*

INCANTATIONS / SPELLS / INVOCATIONS

HECHIZOS / CONJUROS / INVOCACIONES

TLACHIUHTLI / TEXOXALIZTLI / NAHUALLAHTOLLI

Vigilia por mí, Tlacuilo venerable,
ayúdame a ser fiel a mi linaje, las flechas
castigadas por el sol y lavadas por la sombra.
Bendíceme, dile a tus dioses que oren por mí . . .

Look after me, venerable Tlacuilo,
help me to be true to my ancestors, arrows
scorched by the Sun and bathed by Darkness.
Bless me, tell your gods to pray for me . . .

Tino Villanueva

1. PENITENTS

PENITENTES

IN TLAMAHCEUHQUEH

Midnight Water Song
Canción del agua de la medianoche
Yohualnepantlah acuicatl

the eagle's	*el ala del*	*iahtlapal*
wing is	*águila es*	*in cuauhtli*
my fan	*mi abanico*	*nehcacehuaztli*
my people's	*el pasado*	*imihtoloca*
past is	*de mi gente*	*nomacehualpohhuan*
my staff	*es mi bastón*	*nochicuacol*
my pounding	*mi palpitante*	*noyollo*
heart	*corazón*	*in tetecuica*
the only drum	*el único tambor*	*nocel nohuehueuh*
this nightfall	*este crepúsculo*	*inin teotlac*
this sagebrush	*este arbusto de salvia*	*inin xochipalli*
this cedar smoke	*este humo de cedro*	*inin ahuehuetl ipocyo*
tumbleweeds	*las plantas que ruedan*	*huacqui xihuitl*
rattle	*vibran*	*tecuini*
as I sing	*mientras canto*	*inoc nicuica*
of peyote's	*sobre la lluvia*	*ica in peyotl*
flowering rain	*floreciente de peyote*	*ixochiquiyahuitl*
in the desert	*en el desierto*	*nemiuhyan*

Journey

Ruiz de Alarcón (I:4)

In each village there was a large, well-kept courtyard, something like a church, from where the tlamacazqui, the old priest, would send the tlamaceuhque, the penitent, on his rite of passage. Each individual began his pilgrimage by bringing green firewood to this courtyard for the elders, who were distinguished by a long lock of hair. This lock of hair was also a sign among Indians of great captains and warriors called *tlacauhque*.

During the night, the elder, squatting on a low stone seat and holding in his hands a large tecomate (gourd vessel) full of tenexyhetl (tobacco with lime) would then address the tlamaceuhque, ordering him to go to the forest, home of Tlaticpaque, Lord of the Wilderness. The words the elders spoke were:

En cada villa había un bien conservado, largo patio, algo como una iglesia, de donde los tlamacazqui, los viejos sacerdotes, enviaban al tlamaceuhque, el penitente, a su rito de paso. Cada individuo comenzaba su peregrinaje trayendo leña verde a este patio para los ancianos, quienes eran distinguidos por un largo mechón de pelo. Este mechón de pelo era también una distinción entre los grandes capitanes y guerreros indios llamados tlacauhque.

Durante la noche, los ancianos, encuclillados en un asiento de piedra baja y sosteniendo en sus manos un tecomate largo, "vasija de guaje," lleno de tenex yhetl, "tabaco con cal," se dirigían al tlamaceuhque, ordenándole ir al bosque, hogar de Tlalticpaque, señor de la naturaleza salvaje. Las palabras que el anciano decía eran:

xoniciuhtiuh	hurry off	*apúrate*
nocomichic	bottom of my vessel	*fondo de mi vasija*
noxocoyo	my youngest child	*mi hijo menor*
noceuteh	my only one	*mi único*
mazon cana	beware of delaying	*atento a los atrasos*
tlamaahuiltitiuh	somewhere—	*en algún lugar—*
nimitzhixtiyez	I'll be watching you	*estaré vigilándote*
nican niyetlacuitica	here smoking my	*aquí fumando mi pipa*
nitlacuepalotica	tobacco pipe	*de tabaco*
nitlachixtica	keeping up the fire	*manteniendo el fuego*

nitlachixtica	I'm watching you	*te vigilo*
izca	behold!—	*¡mira!—*
nimitzcualtia	I give you	*te doy*
tichuicaz . . .	food to carry . . .	*comida para llevar . . .*
nican nitlachixtica	here I'm watching you—	*aquí estoy cuidándote—*
nOxomoco	I, Oxomoco	*yo, Oxomoco*
niHuehueh	I, the Ancient One	*yo, el Anciano*
niCipactonal	I, Cipactonal	*yo, Cipactonal*

Nehnemi itlahtlauhtiliz

Traveler's Prayer
Oración del viajero

Ruiz de Alarcón (II:1)

nomatca nehuatl	I myself	*Yo mismo*
niQuetzalcoatl	I, Quetzalcoatl	*Yo, Quetzalcoatl*
niMatl	I, the Hand	*Yo, la Mano*
ca nehuatl niYaotl	indeed I, the Warrior	*Yo, ciertamente, el Guerrero*
niMoquequeloatzin	I, the Mocker	*Yo, el Burlón*
atle ipan nitlamati . . .	I respect nothing . . .	*no respeto nada . . .*
tla xihualhuian	come forth	*vengan adelante*
tlamacazque	spirits	*espíritus*
tonatiuh iquizayan	from the sunset	*del atardecer*
tonatiuh icalaquiyan	from the sunrise	*del amanecer*
in ixquichca nemi	anywhere you dwell	*dondequiera que moren*
in yolli	as animals	*como animales*
in patlantinemi	as birds	*como pájaros*
in ic nauhcan	from the four directions	*de las cuatro direcciones*
niquintzatzilia	I call you	*te llamo*
ic axcan yez . . .	to my grip . . .	*a mi agarre . . .*
tla xihuallauh	come forth	*ven adelante*
Ce-Tecpatl	One Flint	*Uno Pedernal*
tezzohuaz	to be stained	*para ser manchado*
titlapallohuaz	with blood	*con sangre*
tla xihuallauh	come forth	*ven adelante*
tlaltecuin	cross my path	*cruza mi camino*

Martín de Luna

Martín de Luna	*Martín de Luna*	*Martín de Luna ye*
110 years old	*de 110 años*	*macuilpohualommahtl*
was arrested	*fue arrestado*	*acxihuitl*
and imprisoned	*y encarcelado*	*in onen inoc oanoc auh omaloc*
for having used	*por haber usado*	*yehica quihtoayah*
incantations	*encantaciones*	*in tlatlahtlauhtiliztli*
before lying down	*antes de recostarse*	*in ayamo oncochiya*
on his petate:	*en su petate:*	*ipan ipetl:*
"tla cuel	*"tla cuel*	*"tla cuel*
nocelopetlatzine	*nocelopetlatzine*	*nocelopetlatzine*
in nauhcampa	*in nauhcampa*	*in nauhcampa*
ticamachalohtoc . . ."	*ticamachalohtoc . . ."*	*ticamachalohtoc . . ."*
"take me	*"llévame*	
jaguar mat into	*tapete jaguar a*	
the four mouths	*las cuatro bocas*	
of your corners . . ."	*de tus esquinas . . ."*	
(take me now	*(llévame ahora*	*(tla cuel xinechmaquixti*
from this cell	*de esta celda*	*itech in tecaltzacualoyan*
and lose me	*y piérdeme*	*auh xinechpolhui*
in the darkness)	*en la oscuridad)*	*itech in yohuayan)*

Day and Night
Día y noche
Tlahcah yohualtica

I bleed	*sangro*	*nizohua*
in silence	*en silencio*	*nahnahuatl*
all alone	*solo*	*zan niyoh*
Martín	*Martín*	*Martín*
Mariana	*Mariana*	*Mariana*
Domingo	*Domingo*	*Domingo*
in fields	*en los campos*	*milpan*
in streets	*en las calles*	*ohtlicapan*
in cells	*en las celdas*	*tecaltzacualoyan*
my fists	*mis puños*	*nomapich*
hit	*golpean*	*quimahuitequi*
walls	*muros*	*in tepantli*
whips	*latigazos*	*in tehuiteconi*
undress	*desnudan*	*quixipehua*
my ribs	*mis costillas*	*in nomicicuil*
from	*de*	*itech*
my mouth	*mi boca*	*nocan*
come out	*salen*	*quizah*
broken teeth	*dientes rotos*	*in poztecqui notlan*
blood	*sangre*	*in nezzo*
butterflies	*mariposas*	*cequin papalomeh*

En el pueblo de Iguala, haciendo yo pesquisa de estos delitos por orden y mandato del Ilmo. Sr. D. Juan de la Serna, arzobispo de México, el año pasado de seiscientos y diez y siete, prendí una india llamada Mariana, sortílega, embustera, curandera de las que llaman Ticitl: esta Mariana declaró que ella sabía y usaba de sus sortilegios y embustes, lo había aprendido de otra india, de Mariana su hermana, y que la dicha hermana no lo había aprendido de persona alguna, sino que le había sido revelado, porque consultando la dicha hermana al ololiuhqui sobre la cura de una llaga vieja, habiéndose embriagado con la fuerza de la bebida llamó al enfermo y sobre unas brasas le sopló la llaga, con que luego sanó la llaga, y tras el soplo inmediatamente se le apareció un mancebo que juzgó ser ángel y la consoló diciéndole: "no tengas pena, cata aquí, te da Dios una gracia y dádiva porque vives pobre y en mucha miseria, para que con esta gracia tengas chile y sal, quiere decir, sustento: curarás las llagas, con sólo lamerlas, y el sarpullido y viruelas, y si no acudieres a esto, morirás"; y tras esto estuvo el dicho mancebo toda la noche dándole una cruz, y crucificándola en ella y clavándole clavos en las manos, y estando dicha india en la cruz, el mancebo le enseñó los modos que sabía de curar, que eran siete o más exorcismos e invocaciones, y que tuvieron quince días continuos luz donde estaba el enfermo da la llaga dicha: debió de ser en veneración de la cura y del portento.

Last year, 1617, while by order and mandate of the Most Reverend Don Juan de la Serna, Archbishop of Mexico, I was investigating certain crimes in the village of Iguala, I arrested an Indian woman named Mariana—a sorceress, charlatan, and healer of the kind they call Ticitl. This Mariana declared she had learned the sorceries and tricks she practiced from her sister. The sister had learned them from no one; they had been revealed to her when consulting the ololiuhqui about the cure of an old wound. Having become intoxicated with the force of the drink, she summoned the sick person and blew on the wound over some hot coals, healing it immediately. Following this cure, there appeared to her a youth whom she judged to be an angel. He consoled her, saying: "Don't worry. Behold, God is granting you a favor and a gift because you live in poverty and misery. Through this favor you will have chile and salt, (that is to say, sustenance). You will cure sores, rashes, and smallpox just be licking them. And if you don't answer this call, you will die." The youth gave her a cross and stayed the night hammering nails through her hands. Then, while the Indian woman was on the cross, he taught her the seven or more exorcisms and incantations he knew for curing. Following this, there were fifteen continuous days of light where the patient with the wound was—this had to be in veneration of the cure and the portent.

Ruiz de Alarcón (I:7)

Heart-Flower
Corazón-Flor Yolloxochitl
Yolloxochitl

it was you	eras tú	oticatca tehhuatl
sister	hermana	tinohueltiuh
your voice	tu voz	motozqui
a seagull	una gaviota	in pipixcan
holding up	sosteniendo	in quinapaloa
the breeze	la brisa	in ehcaxoctli
it was you	eras tú	oticatca tehhuatl
sister	hermana	tinohueltiuh
your breath	tu aliento	mihiyo
forming	formando	quichihua
tiny tears	pequeñas lágrimas	in ixayotontli
on windows	en las ventanas	ipan tlattoyan
it was you	eras tú	oticatca tehhuatl
your ways	tus maneras	in quenin
to climb down	para bajar	cuauhnepanolpan
crosses	cruces	tihualtemoyah
turn things	cambiar	in quenin
around	las cosas	titlamalacachoaya
it was you	eras tú	oticatca tehhuatl
your hands	tus manos	moma
that healed	que curaban	in quinpahtiaya
mended the sick	sanaban	quinpalehuiya
the needy	al enfermo	in cocoxqueh
	al necesitado	in icnopipiltin
it was you	eras tú	oticatca tehhuatl
sister	hermana	tinohueltiuh
your blood	tu sangre	in mezzo
your wounds	tus heridas	in motetequil

Wisdom Seeds

Semillas de sabiduría
Ololiuhqui

   to / *a* / *impampa Barbara García*

seeds	*semillas*	*iachyo*
of wisdom	*de sabiduría*	*in tlamatiliztli*
divine eyes	*ojos divinos*	*inteoix*
of serpents	*de serpientes*	*in cocoah*
teach us	*enséñanos*	*ma quitechmachtican*
to read	*a leer*	*in ticpohuazqueh*
again	*otra vez*	*oc ceppa*
the sky	*el cielo*	*in ihuicatl*
buttons of	*botones de*	*in yahualolli*
the infinite	*la infinita*	*zan ipan*
skirt	*falda*	*ahtlamini*
of stars	*de estrellas*	*in citlalcueitl*
turn us	*transfórmanos*	*ma techmazatilia*
into	*en*	*ma titocuepacan*
hummingbirds	*colibríes*	*in huitzacatzin*
kissing flowers	*besando flores*	*in tennamicxochitl*
lead us	*guíanos*	*ma techhuica*
back	*de regreso*	*oc ceppa*
to the lap	*al regazo*	*in icuexan*
of our Mother	*de nuestra Madre*	*tonantzin*

2. HUNTERS

CAZADORES

IN ANQUEH

Morning Ritual
Ritual matutino
Notequitzin in yohuantzinco

I fold	*doblo*	*niccuelpachoa*
kiss	*beso*	*nictennamiqui*
carry	*cargo*	*niquitqui*
my life	*mi vida*	*in nonemiliz*
inside	*dentro de*	*itech*
my pocket	*mi bolsillo*	*noxiquipilton*

Sucedió que viniendo a orillas de este rio de mi beneficio un indio vecino del pueblo de Santiago, alcanzó otros que se estaban bañando y pasando por ellos, vio en el camino un papel escrito, y cogiolo sin ser visto, y leyéndolo entendió lo que contenía, por haberse criado en mi casa; y así me trajo luego el papel y me refirió lo que contenía, como lo halló y cuyo era. Porque estaba firmado del dueño, que era un sacristán del pueblo de Cuetlaxxochitla, que apenas sabía escribir; mas el demonio le ayudó para que no se perdiese este maleficio. Traído el autor, confesó el delito y dijo habérsele perdido el original, de cuyo autor no supo dar razón.

One day when Francisco de Santiago, an Indian from the village of Santiago, arrived at the banks of a nearby river, he came upon others who were taking a bath. As he passed by them, he saw on the road a piece of paper with writing on it. He picked it up without being seen, and on examining it closer, understood its significance, since he had been reared in my house. He then brought me the paper, and told me what it contained, how he had found it and whose it was. It had been signed by a sacristan in the village of Cuetlaxxochitla who was hardly able to write, but whom the Devil had helped in order that this spell not be lost. When the signator was brought, he confessed the crime and said that he had lost the original, about whose author he could give no information.

Ruiz de Alarcón (II:4)

Tonatiuh itlahtlauhtiliz in ayamo nemohua
Prayer for the Sun Before Traveling
Oración para el sol antes de viajar

Ruiz de Alarcón (II:4)

tla cuel	come	*ven*
tla xihualmohuica	help me	*ayúdame*
Nanahuatzin	Nanahuatzin	*Nanahuatzin*
achtopa niyaz	I'll go first	*iré primero*
achtopa notlatocaz	I'll be on the road first—	*estaré en el camino primero—*
zatepan tiyaz	then you'll go	*después irás*
zatepan totlatocaz	then you'll follow the road	*después seguirás el camino*
achtopa nictlamiltiz	I'll be the first to cross	*seré el primero en cruzar*
in centeotlalotli	all the desert lands	*todas las tierras desiertas*
in cencomolihuic	all the canyon lands	*todas las tierras de cañones*
ca ye niquiczaz	I'll pass swiftly over	*pasaré rápidamente sobre*
in Tlalli Ixcapactzin	the Earth's smooth face—	*la suave cara de la Tierra—*
ahmo nechelehuiz	she won't hinder me	*no me perjudicará*
ca ahmo nelli	no matter what truly lies	*sin importar lo que en verdad yace*
Tlalli Ixcapactzin	on her smooth face	*en su suave cara*
ca zan ilhuicac	up the sky	*arriba en el cielo*
ipan nonyaz	I shall go	*iré*
ipan ninemiz	I shall walk	*caminaré*

Cutting Wood
Cortar leña
Nicuauhtzahtzayana

ahmo	*ahmo*	*ahmo*
tinechelehuiliz	*tinechelehuiliz*	*tinechelehuiliz*
tree	*árbol*	*ticuahuitle*
don't hurt my ax	*no dañes mi hacha*	*macamo xicpitzini notlatequiya*
enjoy it	*disfrútala*	*xicpacqui*
as your mirror	*como tu espejo*	*iuhquin motezcauh*
I offer tobacco	*ofrezco tabaco*	*inquiyahua piciyetl*
for your shin	*por tu espinilla*	*inahuac motlanitz*

Birds
Pájaros
Totomeh

snakes	*serpientes*	*cocoah*
in flight	*en vuelo*	*patlani*

Inic amihua in totomeh
For Hunting Birds
Para cazar pájaros
Ruiz de Alarcón (II:6)

nomatca nehuatl	I myself	*yo mismo*
nIcnopiltzintli	I, Poor Orphan	*yo, Pobre Huérfano*
niCenteotl	I, Centeotl	*yo, Centeotl*
niQuetzalcoatl	I, Quetzalcoatl	*yo, Quetzalcoatl*
onihualla niquintemoz	I've come to seek	*he venido a buscar*
in notlahuan	my uncles	*a mis tíos*
tlamacazque	the spirits	*los espíritus*
ilhuicac pipiltin	the nobles of the sky	*los nobles celestes*
tlaca ye nican oneque	but already sitting here	*pero ya sentados aquí*
in notlahuan	are my uncles	*están mis tíos*
tlamacazque	the spirits	*los espíritus*
Olchipinque	Olchipinque	*Olchipinque*
Olpeyauhque	Olpeyauhque	*Olpeyauhque*
nican nicualhuica	here I bring	*aquí traigo*
in noman ical	my mother's house	*la casa de mi madre*
ihuipil	her huipil	*su huipil*
nica nicehualtiz	here I shall place	*aquí colocaré*
in tlamacazqui	the priest	*al sacerdote*
Ce-Atl Itonal	spirit One Water	*espíritu Uno Agua*
itozcatlan	it shall enter	*se meterá en*
ixillan	the throat	*la garganta*
iciacatlan	the belly	*el vientre*
noconquiz	the armpits	*las axilas*
in nonan	of my mother	*de mi madre*
Chalchiuhcueye	Chalchiuhcueye	*Chalchiuhcueye*
nican niquimonchiaz	here I shall wait	*aquí esperaré*
in notlahuan	for my uncles	*a mis tíos*
tlamacazque	the spirits	*los espíritus*
Olchipinque	Olchipinque	*Olchipinque*
Olpeyauhque	Olpeyauhque	*Olpeyauhque*

Little Toltecs
Toltequitas
Toltecatotontin

"bees are	"las abejas son	"in xicohtin
godly	sirvientes	in tlateomatinih
servants	divinos	innencauh
of the flowers	de las flores	in xochitl
they keep	son	yehhuantin
to themselves	reservadas	ixpinahuapoloah
they make	hacen	quichihuah
the wax	la cera	in xicohcuitlatl
we burn	que quemamos	in tiquitlatiah inic
to our Lord	para nuestro Señor	ticmahuitziah toteucyo
for that	por eso	ic
we love them	las amamos	tictlazoah
we revere them"	las reverenciamos"	ticmahuizoah"
said Miguel	dijo Miguel	oquitoh Miguel
the bee seeker	el que busca las abejas	xicohtlatemoani
after being	después de haber recitado	ca in iztlacahuiloc
tricked to recite	con engaños	inic quitempohuaz
the incantations	los hechizos	in tlatlahtlauhtiliztli
of the beehives	del enjambre	in cuauhnecomitl
he knew better	los conocía mejor	oc hualcah quimatiya
than his Ave Marías	que sus Ave Marías	in ahmo Ave Marías

Inic amihua in mamazah
For Hunting Deer
Para cazar venado

Ruiz de Alarcón (II:9)

ye nonehua nehuatl	I'm leaving	*me estoy yendo*
nIcnopiltzintli	I, Poor Orphan	*yo, Pobre Huérfano*
niCenteotl	I, Centeotl	*yo, Centeotl*
ye nichuica	carrying with me	*llevo conmigo*
Ce-Atl Itonal	the spirit One Water	*el espíritu Uno Agua*
yehuatl inhuan	his bow	*su arco*
iacayo	his arrows	*sus flechas*
in oquichihiuh	made by	*hechos por*
in nonan	my mother	*mi madre*
Tonacacihuatl	Tonacacihuatl	*Tonacacihuatl*
Xochiquetzal	Xochiquetzal	*Xochiquetzal*
cihuatl	the woman	*la mujer*
ompa icatiuh	who wears	*que lleva*
itzapapalotl	obsidian butterflies	*mariposas de obsidiana*
yequene eh nichuicaz	I shall carry back	*traeré*
nota Chicome-Xochitl	my father Seven Flower	*a mi padre Siete Flor*
Piltzinteuctli	Young Lord—	*Joven Señor—*
nicanaco	I've come to take him	*he venido a llevármelo*
nichuicaz	I shall carry him back—	*me lo llevaré cargando—*
ye quichixcaca	already awaiting him	*ya lo está esperando*
nonan Xochiquetzal	is my mother Xochiquetzal	*mi madre Xochiquetzal*
nictemoco can	I've come to seek him	*lo he venido a buscar*
in comolihuic	in ravines	*en los barrancos*
tepayacatl	on mountain summits	*en las cumbres de las montañas*
campa teliuhqui	wherever	*a dondequiera*
quitocatinemi	he goes	*que vaya*
Piltzinteuctli	it's the Young Lord	*es al Joven Señor*
Chicome-Xochitl	Seven Flower	*Siete Flor*
nictemoco can mani	I've come to seek	*a quien he venido a buscar*
inhuan nictemoco	I've come to seek	*he venido a buscar*
Mixcoacihuatl	Mixcoatl's Woman	*a la mujer de Mixcoatl*
in Acaxochtzin	and Reed Flower—	*y a Junco Flor—*
nichuicaz	that's who I shall carry back	*a esos llevaré cargando*

Mazatl tlatzonhuazhuilli
Ensnared Deer
Venado atrapado

Ruiz de Alarcón (II:8)

tlamazcaqui	spirit	*espíritu*
Chicome-Xochitl	Seven Flower	*Siete Flor*
teotlalhua	desert dweller	*morador del desierto*
ye iuhqui	it's all over with	*todo ha terminado*
otititlanihuac	you're a goner	*eres el que se va*
yohualli	in the night	*con la noche*
can in	where is	*¿Dónde está*
Chicome-Xochitl	Seven Flower	*Siete Flor?*
can ca?	where is he?	*¿Dónde está?*
ca opatoloc	and his luck?	*y, ¿su suerte?*
ho ho!	ha ha!	*¡ja, ja!*
tamaloc	he was taken	*fue tomado*
ye iuhqui	it's all over with	*todo ha terminado*

Seven Flower
Siete Flor
Chicome-Xochitl

deer	*ciervo*	*mamazah*
father	*padre*	*itah*
all	*todo*	*mochintin*
stems	*espigas*	*itlacoyo*
pointing	*apuntando*	*quinmahpilhuia*
stars	*estrellas*	*cicitlaltin*

Inic in yolcatl totoco milpan
For Keeping Animals Out of Sown Fields
Para mantener los animales fuera de los campos sembrados
Ruiz de Alarcón (II:11)

As soon as the Indians get to the edge of the sown fields, they remove any broken stalks, ears of corn, spikes of grain, or fallen fruit spoiled by the animals. Then, burning incense as an offering, they say:

Tan pronto como los indios llegan a la orilla de los campos sembrados quitan cualquier tallo roto, mazorcas de maíz, puntas de grano or fruta caída echada a perder por los animales. Después, mientras queman incienso como una ofrenda, dicen:

nomatca nehuatl	I myself	*yo mismo*
niNahualcocelotl	I, the Wizard Jaguar	*yo, el Brujo Jaguar*
onihualla niquimittaz	I've come to find	*he venido a encontrar*
notlahuan	my uncles	*a mis tíos*
tlamacazque	the spirits	*los espíritus*
cozauhque tlamacazque	the yellow spirits	*los espíritus amarillos*
yayauhque tlamacazque	the dark spirits	*los espíritus oscuros*
tlaca!	aha!	*¡ajá!*
nican ohuallaque	here they came	*aquí vinieron*
tlaca!	aha!	*¡ajá!*
nican ocalacque	here they entered	*aquí entraron*
ye no nican quizque	and off they went	*y se fueron*
nican nihualla niquintotocaz	from here I chased them away	*de aquí los corrí*
aocmo nican tlacuazque	they shall never eat here again	*nunca más comerán aquí*
hueca niquintitlani	I am sending them far off	*los mando lejos*
hueca nemizque	and far off they shall stay	*y lejos se quedarán*
nican nichualhuica	here I bring forth	*aquí ofrezco*
in iztac copalli	white copal	*copal blanco*
cozauhque copalli	yellow copal	*copal amarillo*

in niquintlacuiliz	with it I shall mark things away	*con este demarcaré las cosas*
in notlahuancan	from my uncles	*de mis tíos*
tlamacazque	the spirits	*los espíritus*
cozauhque tlamacazque	the yellow spirits	*los espíritus amarillos*
yayauhque tlamacazque	the dark spirits	*los espíritus oscuros*
nota	o, father	*oh padre*
Nahui-Acatl	Four Reed	*Cuatro Junco*
Milintica	Flaming One!	*¡El Flameante!*

Inhuicpa in azcameh ahcemeleh
Against Unruly Ants
Contra hormigas revoltosas
Ruiz de Alarcón (II:13)

If the ants do not respond to the conjurer's pleas by leaving, he carries out this threat, destroying their houses by pouring a quantity of water onto the anthill and sprinkling the outer edge and circumference with his so venerated piciete ("tobacco").

Si las hormigas no responden, a la súplica del conjurador, y no se van, él cumplirá su amenaza, destruirá sus casas regando agua en su hormiguero y salpicando en la orilla externa y la circunferencia su venerado piciete ("tabaco").

tla cuel!	come now!	*¡ven ahora!*
Chalchiuhcueye	Mother Water	*Madre Agua*
tle in ai	what are the ants	*¿qué hacen las hormigas*
in popotecatl?	doing around?	*por aquí?*
tla xiquimpoploti	wipe them out	*bárrelas*
ahmo nechtlacamati	they don't obey me	*no me obedecen*
cuix nelhuayoticate?	are they perhaps	*¿están quizá*
ye cuahuitl tichuica	rooted?	*enraizadas?*
tictlaochtitiquiza	you uproot trees	*tú desarraigas árboles*
in hueca ixtlahuacan	quickly wash them	*rápidamente los acarreas*
teohixtlahuacan nepantla	away to the far-off	*hasta las lejanas*
toconxiccahua	dusty plains	*planicies polvosas*
cuix annelhuayoticate?	are you perhaps rooted?	*¿estás quizá enraizado?*
tla cuel!	come now!	*¡ven ahora!*
Xoxouqui Tlamacazqui	Green Spirit	*Espíritu Verde*
Xiuhpapatlantzin	Tobacco	*Tabaco*
tle axtica?	why delay more?	*¿por qué tardarse más?*
tla xocontocati	chase them away	*corretéalas*
in popotecatl	close their town	*cierra su pueblo*

Intechpa in tlalocuiltin in ayamo michmalo
To Earthworms Before Fishing with a Hook
A los gusanos de tierra antes de pescar con un gancho
Ruiz de Alarcón (II:15)

tla xihualhuian	help me	*ayúdame*
in Iztac-Tlamacazqui	White Spirit	*Espíritu Blanco*
ye nican ihuan	soon here	*pronto aquí*
timonahuahtequiz	you will embrace	*abrazarás*
in tlatlauhqui chichimecatl	the red chichimec	*al chichimeca rojo*
cuix zan ce nicnotza?	am I calling just one?	*¿sólo he de llamar a uno?*
ca zan mocha nicnotza	indeed all of them I call:	*ciertamente a todos llamo:*
in piltontli	the child fish	*el niño pez*
in huehuentzin	the man fish	*el hombre pez*
ilmatzin	the woman fish—	*la mujer pez—*
in anenecuilcan chaneque	dwellers of meanders	*habitantes de meandros*

Spirits of the Forest
Espíritus del bosque
Cuauhtlah tlamacazqueh

when the last	*cuando las últimas*	*in ye iuhqui in yequeneh*
rainforests	*selvas tropicales*	*in ayauhtic cuauhtlah*
become zoos	*sean ya zoológicos*	*mochihuaz totocalco*
will there be	*¿acaso habrá filas*	*cuix ticempantitiyazqueh*
lines to the pond	*al tanque de sueños*	*inahuac in michacaxitl*
of wild dreams?	*del mundo salvaje?*	*in ahtlacacah temictli?*
who will dare	*¿quién se atreverá*	*aquin motlahpaloaz*
disturb	*cuestionar este orden*	*inic quelleltiz inin*
this order of lies?	*de verdades falsas?*	*tlatecpantli in tlahtolpictli?*
must the last	*¿debe la última*	*cuix monequi*
eagle die	*águila real morir*	*miquiz petlacalco*
in a cage?	*enjaulada?*	*cecen cuauhtli?*
what will take	*¿qué reemplazará*	*tlein*
the place of	*a nuestros*	*quixiptlahtiz*
our spirits?	*espíritus?*	*notlamacazcauh?*

3. FARMERS

CAMPESINOS

IN MILLAHCAH

Sólo un dios tenían.
         Su nombre era Quetzalcoatl.
Su sacerdote,
         su nombre era también Quetzalcoatl.
Todo lo de Quetzalcoatl
         se los decía su sacerdote Quetzalcoatl:
Quetzalcoatl nada exige
         sino serpientes, sino mariposas
que vosotros debéis ofrecerle
         que vosotros debéis sacrificarle.

They only had one God.
         His name was Quetzalcoatl.
Their priest,
         his name was also Quetzalcoatl.
The priest Quetzalcoatl would tell them
         everything about Quetzalcoatl:
Quetzalcoatl demands nothing
         but serpents and butterflies,
which you must offer him
         which you must sacrifice to him.

Ancient Nahuatl poem, quoted in Quetzalcoatl *by Ernesto Cardenal*

First Offering
Primera ofrenda
In achtopa huentli

ourselves	*nosotros mismos*	*ticateh nehhuantin*
molded out	*moldeados de*	*titocopinah*
of huauhtli	*huauhtli*	*in huauhtli*
the first crop	*la primera cosecha*	*in achtopa pixquitl*
smiling	*sonríe*	*ixhuetzca*
everywhere	*en todos lados*	*nohuiyan*

Honeywater
Aguamiel
Necuatl

in its heart	*en su corazón*	*ihtec iyolloh*
the maguey	*el maguey*	*in metl*
weeps	*llora*	*choca*
sweats	*suda*	*mitonia*
streams	*corrientes*	*in acanactli*
of sweet	*de dulces*	*in tzopelic*
tears	*gotas*	*choquiztli*
and drops	*y lágrimas*	*achipintli*

Clouds
Nubes
Mixitl

mountains	*las montañas*	*tepemeh*
dreaming	*soñándose*	*quitemiquih*
up the sky	*el cielo*	*in ilhuicatl*

De esta metáfora de las siete culebras usan siempre en estos conjuros por el maíz, y es o por los racimos atados de las mazorcas, o por las cañas en que se da, que de ordinario los siembran y nacen de siete en siete, o por las hileras del maíz en la misma mazorca que suelen asemejar las culebras tendidas de diferentes colores.

This metaphor of the seven snakes is always used in these incantations for corn, and it is either because of the tied bunches of the ears or because of the stalks of which it is produced, since they usually sow them and they are born seven by seven or because of the rows of kernels on the ear which usually resemble the snakes stretched out in different colors.

Ruiz de Alarcón (III:2)

Seven Snake
Siete Serpiente
Chicome-Coatl

corn stalks	*las milpas*	*cintopilli*
are upright	*son serpientes*	*ca coatl*
snakes	*erguidas*	*in ihcac*
corn ears	*los elotes*	*cintli*
rattle	*cascabelean*	*cacalaca*
in the wind	*con el viento*	*ehecaticpac*

Snake Wheel
Rueda víbora
Temalacacoatl

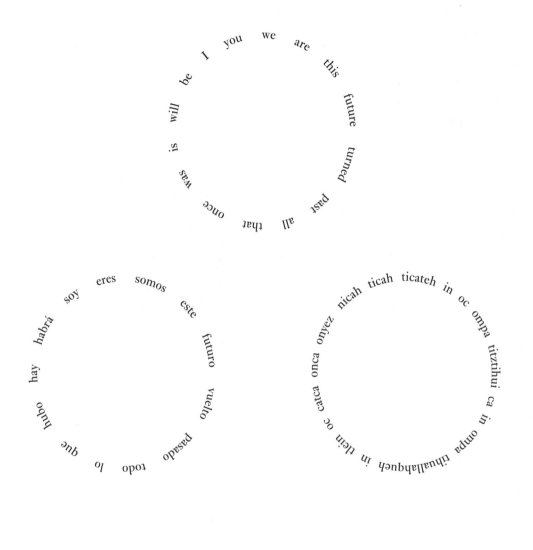

Calendar Keepers
Guardianes del calendario
Tonalpouhqueh

rattlesnakes	*las víboras*	*in chiyauhcoatl*
renew	*de cascabel*	*moyancuillia*
themselves	*se renuevan*	*cecexiuhtica*
each year	*cada año*	
by shedding	*dejando atrás*	*in quixipehuaya*
their skins	*su vieja piel*	*iehuayo*
by adding	*y añadiendo*	*in quiza*
a new ring	*otro cascabel*	*yancuic cuechtli*
they trace	*marcando así*	*quitexxinepanoa*
the shining	*el luminoso paso*	*in pepetlacac*
path of our	*de las temporadas*	*ohtli in*
rainy seasons	*nuestras de lluvias*	*toxopaniz*

Thunder

Trueno
Cuacualachtli

Tlaloc's laughter	*la carcajada de Tlaloc*	*Tlaloc ihuetzquiliz*
from afar	*desde lejos*	*huehca caquizti*

Rainbow
Arcoíris
Ayauhcozamalotl

seven	*siete*	*chichicomeh*
snakes	*víboras*	*cocoah*
giving	*dando*	*huel*
thanks	*gracias*	*motlazohmati*

Water Spirits
Espíritus de agua
Atlamacazqueh

these rivers	*estos ríos*	*inin atoyaatl*
flow deep	*fluyen dentro*	*meya centlani*
inside	*en lo profundo*	*tlalihtic*
well uphill	*brotan cuesta arriba*	*moloni tlehcotiuh*
steam off	*el vapor se desprende*	*apoctli mocuepa*
volcanoes	*de los volcanes*	*tletepeticpac*

Inic aquilo in cintli
For Planting Corn
Para sembrar maíz

Ruiz de Alarcón (III:4)

nomatca nehuatl	I myself	*yo mismo*
nitlamacazqui	Spirit in Flesh	*Espíritu en la Encarnado*
tla xihualhuian	hear me, Tonacacihuatl	*escúchame, Tonacacihuatl*
nohueltiuh	elder sister	*hermana mayor*
Tonacacihuatl	Lady of Our Flesh	*Señora de Nuestro Sustento*
tla xihualhuian	hear me, Tlalteuctli	*escúchame, Tlalteuctli*
Tlalteuctli	Mother Earth	*Madre Tierra*
yo nomacpalco	on your open hand	*en la palma de tu mano*
nocontlalia	I'm setting down	*estoy poniendo*
nohueltiuh	my elder sister	*a mi hermana mayor*
Tonacacihuatl	Tonacacihuatl	*Tonacacihuatl*
ahmo timopinauhtiz	don't shame yourself	*no te avergüences*
ahmo tihuxcapehuaz	don't grumble	*no te resongas*
ahmo tihuexcatlalacoz	don't laugh at us	*no te rías de nosotros*
cuix quin moztla	tomorrow	*mañana*
cuix quin huiptla	or the day after	*o el día siguiente*
in ixco icpac nitlachiaz	I want to see again	*quiero ver otra vez*
in nohueltiuh	the face of my elder sister	*el rostro de mi hermana mayor*
Tonacacihuatl	Tonacacihuatl	*Tonacacihuatl*
niman iciuhca	let her stand	*déjala que salga*
in tlalticpac hualquitzaz	on the ground	*de la tierra*
in nicmahuizoz	I shall greet	*saludaré*
in nictlapaloz	I shall honor	*honraré*
in nohueltiuh	my elder sister	*a mi hermana mayor*
Tonacacihuatl	Tonacacihuatl	*Tonacacihuatl*

Inic motlatia in cintli
For Storing Corn
Para almacenar maíz
Ruiz de Alarcón (III:5)

nomatca nehuatl	I myself	*yo mismo*
nitlamacazqui	Spirit in Flesh	*Espíritu Encarnado*
tla xihualhuian	come forth	*ven adelante*
nohueltiuh	elder sister	*hermana mayor*
Tonacacihuatl	Lady of Our Flesh	*Señora de Nuestro Carne*
ye nimitzoncahuaz in	soon I shall place you	*pronto te colocaré*
nochalchiuhcontzinco	inside my jade jar	*dentro de mi vasija de jade*
nauhcampa xitlaquitzqui	hold up the four directions	*venera las cuatro direcciones*
ahmo timpoinauhtiz	don't shame yourself	*no te avergüences*
motech nihiyocuiz	you shall be my breath	*tú serás mi aliento*
motech niceceyaz	you shall be my cure	*tú serás mi cura*
in nlcnopiltzintli	for me, Poor Orphan	*para mí, Pobre Huérfano*
in niCenteotl	for me, Centeotl	*para mí, Centeotl*
in tinohueltiuh	you, my elder sister	*tú, hermana mayor*
tiTonacacihuatl	you, Tonacacihuatl	*tú, Tonacacihuatl*

Inic aquilo in camohtli
For Planting Camotes
Para sembrar camotes

Ruiz de Alarcón (III:7)

This spell is spoken directly to the sun after the roots and stems have been prepared for planting.

Este conjuro es dirigido directamente al sol después de que las raíces y los tallos hayan sido preparados para ser sembrados.

nomatca nehuatl	I myself	*yo mismo*
nIcnopiltzintli	I, Poor Orphan	*yo, Pobre Huérfano*
niCenteotl	I, Centeotl	*yo, Centeotl*
tla xihualhuian	come forth	*ven adelante*
notla	uncle	*tío*
tlamacazqui Nanahuatzin	spirit Nanahuatzin	*espíritu Nanahuatzin*
ca nican niquilpia	here I tie up	*aquí amarro*
nometzcuauhyo	my thigh	*mi muslo*
nictoca	I plant it	*lo siembro*
tla xihualhuian	come forth	*ven adelante*
notla Nanahuatzin	uncle Nanahuatzin	*tío Nanahuatzin*
ca nican niquilpia	here I tie up	*aquí amarro*
notzontecon	my head	*mi cabeza*
ca ica noconilpia	I tie it up	*la amarro*
in nohueltiuh	to my sister	*a mi hermana*
in tetencuacua xochitl	the lip-biting flower	*la flor que muerde labios*
temacochihuia xochitl	the embracing flower	*la flor que abraza*
itetzinco nihiouiz	with her I shall breathe	*con ella respiraré*
itetzinco nipahtiz	with her I shall heal	*con ella sanaré*
nicnotlacatzintli	I, just a poor person	*yo, sólo un pobre*

Song for Tortillas
Canto a las tortillas
Tlaxcalcuicatl

I go on	*yo sigo*	*niquinotzatiuh*
calling out	*nombrando*	*nocih*
nana to	*Nana*	*inic huitz*
the Earth	*a la Tierra*	*tlalticpac*
feeding on	*alimentándome*	*niccua in*
the subversive	*del subversivo*	*ahtecacqui cuicatl*
canto sown	*canto sembrado*	*in oquipixohqueh*
by the ancient ones	*por los antiguos*	*in huehhueyintin*
inside	*dentro de*	*ihtic*
the humblest	*las más humildes*	*in mocnomatini*
tortillas	*tortillas*	*tlaxcalli*
of life	*de la vida*	*in tlacanemiliztli*

Ode to Tomatoes
Oda a los jitomates
Xitomacuicatl

they make	*hacen*	*yehhuantin*
friends	*amigos*	*moteicniuhtiah*
anywhere	*dondequiera*	*zazo canah*
red	*sonrisas*	*tlatlahuic*
smiles	*coloradas*	*huetzquiztli*
in salads	*en ensaladas*	*quilnehneltech*
tender	*tiernos*	*yamactic*
young	*jóvenes*	*xochtic*
generous	*generosos*	*tetlauhtianimeh*
hot	*bailarinas*	*macehuanimeh*
salsa	*de salsa*	*in cococ*
dancers	*calientita*	*xitomamolli*
round	*cardenales*	*yahualtic*
cardinals	*rechonchos*	*cuacuacuiltin*
of the kitchen	*de la cocina*	*in tlecuilli*
hard	*¡difícil*	*ohuih*
to imagine	*imaginarnos*	*ipan macho*
cooking	*cocinar*	*in tlapahuazcalli*
without	*sin antes*	*intlacahmo*
first asking	*pedirles*	*achto*
their blessings!	*su bendición!*	*ceyah*

Urban Villagers
Aldeanos urbanos
Altepetlacah

hummingbirds	*los colibríes*	*in huitzilin*
consoling	*consuelan*	*quiyollalia*
the flowers	*las flores*	*in xochitl*
of the avenues	*de las avenidas*	*in ohtli*

Drought
Sequía
Huaccayotl

despite	*a pesar*	*intlanel*
dry	*de años*	*huaqui*
years	*secos*	*in xihuitl*
siempre	*always*	*cemihcac*
verde	*green*	*xoxouhqui*
inside	*por dentro*	*teihtic*

4. LOVERS

AMANTES

IN TLAZOHTLALIZEHQUEH

ya sea que seamos
hispanos, mexicanos
somos más indios

whether we are
Hispanics, Mexicans
we're really Indians

Agueda Martínez, citada en una película producida por el cineasta Moctezuma Esparza
Agueda Martínez, quoted in a film produced by filmmaker Moctezuma Esparza

Potent Seeds
Semillas potentes
Achtli huelitic

few corn	*unos pocos*	*quezqui*
kernels	*granos de maíz*	*tlaolli*
enough	*suficientes*	*ye cualli*
to turn	*para*	*quicualtilia*
anger	*deshacer*	*in cualantli*
around	*el enojo*	*polihui*

Una de las cosas de que usan por medicina a que atribuyen parte del efecto, son unos granos de maíz que tienen su asiento en principio y nacimiento de la espiga o mazorca, y tales granos tienen las puntillas contrarias al nacimiento, al revés y a la parte contraria que las demás de la dicha mazorca, y a estas contrariedades atribuyen el efecto contrario en la inclinación y voluntad en cuanto a la afinación y odio. A estos granos de maíz aplican la segunda parte de este medio, que son las palabras con que, a su juicio, conjurando los maíces, les dan nueva fuerza y virtud para conseguir el efecto del trueque que pretenden. . . . Hecho este conjuro para aplicar la medicina, moliendo el maíz, conjurado, hacen de él alguna bebida al uso de esta tierra, como es atole y cacao, y dánselo a beber al que pretenden trueque la voluntad o afecto.

Among the things they use for medicine against anger are the corn kernels that are located at the beginning and root of the spike or ear. These kernels have their points contrary to their root—backwards and in the opposite direction to the rest of that particular ear. It is to this inverted position that the Indians attribute the contrary effect the incantation and spell have on affection and hatred. To the corn kernels they apply these words, which they believe give the kernels added strength and power and allow them to effect the change they seek. . . . After the conjured corn has been ground, it is administered orally, as either atole or chocolate, to the person whose will or affection they want to change.

Ruiz de Alarcón (IV:1)

Ihuicpa in tecualan
Against Anger
Contra el enojo

Ruiz de Alarcón (IV:1)

tla xihualhuian	come forth	*ven adelante*
Tlazopilli	Tlazopilli	*Tlazopilli*
Centeotl	Centeotl	*Centeotl*
ticcehuiz	you will calm down	*calmarás*
cozauhque yollotli	the yellow heart	*el corazón amarillo*
quizaz	the green anger	*el enojo verde*
xoxouhqui tlahuelli	the yellow anger	*el enojo amarillo*
cozauhqui tlahuelli	will come out	*saldrán*
nicquixtiz	I shall make it leave	*haré que se vaya*
nictotocaz	I shall chase it away—	*lo correré—*
nitlamacazqui	I, Spirit in Flesh	*yo, Espíritu Encarnado*
niNahualteuctli	I, the Enchanter	*yo, el Encantador*
niquitiz tlamazcazqui	through this drink	*con esta bebida*
Pahtecatl	Medicine Spirit	*Espíritu Medicina*
yollocuepcatzin	will change this heart	*cambiará este corazón*

Home Spirit
Espíritu de casa
In calli iyollo

you lock	*cierras*	**tinquintzacua**
windows	*ventanas*	**mocoyonca**
doors	*puertas*	**motlatzacuil**
but I'm	*pero estoy*	**auh nicah**
inside:	*dentro:*	**iihtic:**
am you	*soy tú*	**nitehhuatl**

Inic tecochtlazalo
To Cast Sleep
Para conjurar el sueño

Ruiz de Alarcón (II:2)

nomatca nehuatl	I myself	yo mismo
niMoyohualitoatzin	I, the One-Called-Night	yo, el Que-Se-Llama-Noche
in ic nehuatl	because I am	porque soy
in ic Chiucnauh Topan	from the Nine Topan	del Nueve Topan
in icuac . . .	at this time . . .	en este momento . . .
tla xihualhuian	come forth	ven adelante
in Temicxoch	Dream-Flower—	Flor-de-Sueño—
in cuac	at this time	en este momento
in ic nicanato	I went to take	fui por mi hermana
in nohueltiuh	my elder sister	mayor
Chiucnauh Topan	to the Nine Topan	al Nueve Topan
nitlamacazqui	I, Spirit in Flesh	yo, Espíritu Encarnado
in nohueltiuh	whose sister	cuya hermana
Xochiquetzal	Xochiquetzal	Xochiquetzal
in ic cenca quipiaya	was so guarded	estuvo tan custodiada
in tlamacazque	by the priests	por los sacerdotes
in mochintin in cuauhtin	by all the eagles	por todas las águilas
in ocelome	and the jaguars	y los jaguares
in ayac huel calaquiya	no one could enter	que nadie podía entrar
in ic nictzatzili	shouting I called	gritando llamé
in cochiztli	for sleep to come	al sueño para que viniera
in ic Chiucnauh-Mictlan	all they went	y todos ellos fueron
yaque	to Nine Mictlan	a Nueve Mictlan
in ic nehuatl	since I am	ya que soy
niXolotl	the Double	el Doble
niCapanilli	the Joint Cracker	el Truenanudillos
in zan tlalhuiz	who mindlessly	quien sin pensar
nohuiyan nitzatzi	cries out everywhere	grita por todas partes
tla xihuallauh	come forth	ven adelante
tlamacazqui Ce-Tecpatl	spirit One Flint—	espíritu Uno Pedernal—

tla xoconmatiti	go and see	*ve y fíjate*
in nohueltiuh cuix ococh	in my elder sister's sleeping	*si mi hermana mayor duerme*
ye nicquixtitiuh	I'm going to take her away	*me la voy a llevar*
in ic ahmo nechelehuizque	and her brothers	*y sus hermanos*
yehuantin	won't harm me	*no me lastimarán*
ixquichtin ioquichtihuan	none of her men	*ninguno de sus hombres*
ahmo nechelehuizque	will harm me	*me dañará*
in ic ye nichuicaz	when I take her	*cuando me la lleve*
in Chiucnauh-Mictlan	to Nine Mictlan	*a Nueve Mictlan*
in oncan nichuicaz	I will take her to	*me la llevaré*
tlalli inepantla	the center of the earth	*al centro de la tierra*
in ic oncan nicmacatiuh	I will deliver her to	*se la entregaré*
in Moyohualitoatzin	the One-Called-Night	*al Que-Se-Llama-Noche*
in ic nauhcan	from the four directions	*de las cuatro direcciones*
niccuepaz	I will bring her back	*la traeré de regreso*
in ic ahmo quimatiz	and she won't feel a thing	*y no sentirá nada*
nehuatl	I am	*yo soy*
ni Yaotl	the Warrior	*el Guerrero*
niMoquequeloatzin	the Mocker—	*el Burlón—*
in ic ye nicahahuiltiz	soon I shall give her pleasure	*pronto le daré placer*
in ic ye niquincuepaz	soon I shall change the others	*pronto cambiaré a los otros*
niquinmiccauepaz	put them to sleep as dead	*los pondré a dormir como muertos*
in ni Yaotl	I, the Warrior	*yo, el Guerrero*
niMoquequeloatzin	I, the Mocker—	*yo, el Burlón—*
in ic ye niquinmacaz	soon I shall do this to them	*pronto haré esto a ellos*
in ic yohuallahuanazque	and all shall be drunk with night	*y todos estarán borrachos con la noche*

Inic quixinilo in cochtlazaliztli
To Undo the Sleep Spell
Para deshacer el conjuro del sueño

Ruiz de Alarcón (II:2)

in ic niquimanatiuh	I'm going to take them back	*los voy a regresar*
tlalli inepantla	from the center of the Earth	*del centro de la Tierra*
in ic nauhcampa	from the four directions:	*de las cuatro direcciones:*
in ahmo nelli in	it's not true that	*no es verdad que*
no niquincuepa	I changed them—	*los he cambiado—*
in ahmo cochiya	they were not sleeping	*no estaban durmiendo*
in ahmo oyaca	they did not go	*no fueron a*
ChiucnauhMictlan	to Nine Mictlan	*Nueve Mictlan*
in ahmo nelli oquinhuicac	neither did the One-Called-Night	*tampoco el Que-Se-Llama-Noche*
in Moyohualitoatzin	truly take them away	*en verdad se los llevó*
ea!	come on!	*¡vengan!*
ye niquincuepa	I've already brought them back	*ya los he traído de regreso*
in yehuatl in Temicxoch	from their Dream-Flower—	*de su Flor-de-Sueño—*
in nehuatl	I am	*yo soy*
in ni Yohuallahuantzin	the Night-Drinker	*el Bebedor-de-la-Noche*

Inic namico tetlazohtlaliz
For Finding Affection
Para encontrar afecto
Ruiz de Alarcón (IV:2)

Tezcatepec	on Mirror Mountain	*en la Montaña Espejo*
nenamicoyan	the place of encounters	*el lugar de encuentros*
nicihuanotza	I call for a woman	*llamo a una mujer*
nicihuacuica	I sing out for her	*canto para ella*
nonnentlamati	crying up	*lloro en alto*
nihualnentlamati	crying down	*lloro en bajo*
ye noconhuica	already at my side	*ya a mi lado*
in nonhueltiuth	my elder sister	*mi hermana mayor*
in Xochiquetzal	Xochiquetzal	*Xochiquetzal*
Ce-Coatl ica	with One Serpent	*con Uno Serpiente*
apantihuitz	as her mantle	*como su túnica*
Ce-Coatl ica	with One Serpent	*con Uno Serpiente*
cuitlalpitihuitz	as her belt	*como su cinturón*
tzonilpitihuitz	as ribbon in her hair	*como listón en su cabellera*
ye yalhua	yesterday	*ayer*
ye huiptla	the day before	*el día anterior*
ica nichoca	I wept	*sollocé*
ica ninentlamati	I cried	*lloré*
ca mach nelli teotl	she is a true goddess	*es una verdadera diosa*
ca mach nelli mahuiztic	she is true power	*es el poder verdadero*
cuix quin moztla	tomorrow?	*¿mañana?*
cuix quin huiptla	the day after?	*¿el día después?*
niman aman	right now?	*¡ahora mismo!*
nomatca nehuatl	I myself	*yo mismo*
niTelpochtli	I, the Youth	*yo, el Joven*
niYaotl	I, the Warrior	*yo, el Guerrero*

no nitonac	I, sunshine	*yo, rayo de sol*
no nitlathuic	I, dawn	*yo, amanecer*
cuix zan cana onihualla	risen from nowhere?	*¿resucitado de la nada?*
cuix zan cana onihualquiz	I have risen,	*yo he resucitado,*
ompa onihualla	I was born	*nací*
ompa onihualquiz . . .	of a woman's flower . . .	*de la flor de una mujer . . .*

The words that belong here, even though somewhat disguised, are omitted out of concern for modest and chaste ears.

Las palabras que pertenecen aquí, de alguna manera molestas, han sido omitidas por la consideración de oídos modestos y castos.

ca mach nelli teotl	she is a true goddess	*es diosa verdadera*
ca mach nelli mahuiztic	she is true power	*es el poder verdadero*
cuix quin moztla	will I find her	*¿la encontraré*
cuix quin huiptla	tomorrow?	*mañana?*
niquittaz	the day after?	*¿el día después?*
niman aman	right now!	*¡ahora mismo!*
nomatca nehuatl	I myself	*yo mismo*
niTelpochtli	I, the Youth	*yo, el Joven*
niYaotl	I, the Warrior	*yo, el Guerrero*
cuix nelli niYaotl	am I truly warlike?	*¿soy en verdad como la guerra?*
ahmo nelli niYaotl	I am not truly at war—	*no estoy en verdad en guerra—*
zan niCihuayotl	I'm of a woman's womb	*vengo del útero de una mujer*

For Love

Para el amor

Ipampa in notlazohtlaliz

enchanted	*encantadoras*	**tlahtolli**
words	*palabras*	**nahualhuiani**
at dawn	*al amanecer*	**tlahuizcalpan**
a handful	*un manojo*	**itlalpil**
of flowers	*de flores*	**xochitl**
and stars	*y estrellas*	**auh citlalin**

Nature
Naturaleza
In yoliliztli

the nature	*la naturaleza*	*in iyeliz*
of poetry's	*de la naturaleza*	*xochicuicatl*
nature	*de la poesía*	*ca in yoliliztli*
the nature	*la naturaleza*	*in iyeliz*
of religion's	*de la naturaleza*	*teoyotl*
nature	*de la religión*	*ca in yoliliztli*
the nature	*la naturaleza*	*in iyeliz*
of nature's	*de la naturaleza*	*yoliliztli*
nature	*de la naturaleza*	*ca in yoliliztli*

Inic maltia
For Bathing
Para bañarse

Ruiz de Alarcón (IV:3)

tla xihualhuian	come forth	*ven adelante*
Ayahuitl Itzon	Mist Hair	*Cabello de Bruma*
Poctli Itzon	Smoke Hair	*Cabello de Humo*
Nonan	Mother of mine	*Madre mía*
Chalchiuhcueye	Chalchiuhcueye	*Chalchiuhcueye*
Iztac Cihuatl	White Woman	*Mujer Blanca*
tla xihualhuian	come forth	*vengan adelante*
in anTlazolteteo	Goddesses of Filth	*Diosas de la Inmundicia*
in tiCuaton	you, Cuaton	*tú, Cuaton*
in tiCaxxoch	you, Caxxoch	*tú, Caxxoch*
in tiTlahui	you, Tlahui	*tú, Tlahui*
in tiXapel	you, Xapel	*tú, Xapel*
xinechitztimamaniqui	remove	*remueve*
yayauhqui tlazolli	the dark filth	*la inmundicia oscura*
iztac tlazolli	the white filth	*la inmundicia blanca*
xoxouhqui tlazolli	the green filth	*la inmundicia verde*
onihualla	I have come	*he venido*
nitlamacazqui	I, Spirit in Flesh	*yo, Espíritu Encarnado*
niNahualteuctli	I, the Enchanter	*yo, el Encantador*
Xoxouhqui Tlaloc	Green Tlaloc	*Tlaloc Verde*
Iztac Tlaloc	White Tlaloc:	*Tlaloc Blanco:*
ma noca	beware	*cuídate*
tehuahti	of rising against me	*de levantarte en mi contra*
ma noca	beware	*cuídate*
timilacatzoti	of turning against me	*de volverte en mi contra*
nomatca nehuatl	I myself	*yo mismo*
nitlamacazqui	I, Spirit in Flesh	*yo, Espíritu Encarnado*
niNahualteuctli	I, the Enchanter	*yo, el Encantador*

Seer
Visionario
Ontlachiyani

I sweep	*barro*	*nicochpana*
and clean	*y limpio*	*auh nicpohpohua*
my house	*mi casa*	*nocal*
I burn	*quemo*	*nictlatia*
the trash	*la basura*	*in tlachpanalli*
get rid	*me deshago*	*nicquixtia*
of obstacles	*de obstáculos*	*in tlaelleltiliztli*
my house	*mi casa*	*nocalco*
now has	*ahora no tiene*	*aocmo cah*
no walls	*ni muros*	*tepantli*
no anger	*ni ira*	*cualaniliztli*
no sorrow	*ni pena*	*auh ellelli*
I am resting—	*descanso—*	*ninocehuia—*
my hamaca	*mi hamaca*	*nochitah*
is a canoe	*una canoa*	*ca acalli*
crossing	*que cruza*	*citlalinicue*
the Milky Way	*la Vía Láctea*	*ipan nipano*

Visions
Visiones
Tlachiyaliztli

at night	*de noche*	*yohualtica*
I see	*yo veo*	*nitlaitta*
by ear	*a oídas*	*nonacaztica*
by hand	*a tientas*	*nomatica*
by heart	*a corazonadas*	*noyollohtica*

Listen
Escucha
Xitlacaquican

every	*cada*	*cecen*
landscape	*paisaje*	*ittaliztli*
a wondrous	*una historia*	**mahuiztic**
story	*maravillosa*	**tetlalhuillo**

Oracle
Oráculo
Achtopaihtoani

"it's me"	*"soy yo"*	*"ca nehhuatl"*
I say	*digo*	*niquihtoa*
"it's us"	*"somos nosotros"*	*"ca nehhuantin"*
rocks echo	*el eco de riscos*	*tetepeh caquiztih*

5. DIVINERS

ADIVINOS

IN TLACIUHQUEH

. . . para adivinar por las manos no lo hacen por las rayas, costumbre y superstición de gitanos, sino midiendo el medio brazo izquierdo desde el codo a la punta de los dedos con la mano derecha, tendiendo el palmo por el medio brazo . . .

. . . in divining with the hands, the Indians don't read palms—the custom and superstition of the Gypsies—but measure the left forearm from the elbow to the fingertips, stretching out the span of the right hand on the forearm . . .

Ruiz de Alarcón (V:1)

Achtopaihtolo matica
Divining with the Hands
Adivinar con las manos
Ruiz de Alarcon (V:1)

nomatca nehuatl	I myself	*yo mismo*
nitlamacazqui	I, Spirit in Flesh	*yo, Espíritu Encarnado*
ninahuealtecutli	I, the Enchanter	*yo, el Conjurador*
niXolotl	I, the Double	*yo, el Doble*
tla cuel he!	help now!	*¡ayuda ahora!*
tla xihualhuian	come forth	*ven adelante*
tlamacazqui	spirit	*espíritu*
Chiucnauhtlatecapanilli	Nine-Times-Crushed-One	*el Nueve-Veces-Destrozado*
Chiucnauhtlatlamatelolli	Nine-Times-Crumbled-One	*el Nueve-Veces-Desmoronado*
Chiucnauhtlatezohtzontli	Nine-Times-Powdered-One	*el Nueve-Veces-Pulverizado*
Xoxouhqui Tlamacazqui	Green Spirit	*Espíritu Verde*
nonan	mother	*madre*
nota	father of mine	*padre mío*
Citlalcueye ipiltzin	son of the Milky Way	*hijo de la Vía Láctea*
nonan Ce-Tochtli Aquetzimani	my mother One Rabbit Supine	*mi madre Uno Conejo Supino*
Tzotzotlactoc	you who are resplendent	*tú que eres resplandeciente*
Tezcatl in zan hualpopocatimani	the Smoking Mirror of Earth	*el Espejo Humeante de la Tierra*
ayac tlatlacoz	none shall fail	*nadie fallará*
ayac huexcapehuaz	none shall grumble	*nadie se quejará*
ca nictaennamiqui	now I kiss	*ahora beso*
Macuiltonaleca	the five solar spirits	*los cincos espíritus solares*
oniquinhaulhuicac	I've brought forth	*que he traído*

Here the diviner puts his hands together, as if praying, crosses one thumb over the other, and kisses them.

Aquí el adivino junta sus manos, como si rezara, cruza los pulgares y los besa.

tla xihualhuian	come on	*vengan*
noquichtihuan	elder brothers of mine	*hermanos mayores míos*
in Macuiltonaleque	five solar spirits each	*cada uno cinco espíritus solares*
cemithualeque	one-courtyard-owners	*dueños-de-un-patio-real*
tzoneptzitzinme	pearly-headed ones	*los de cabezas nacaradas*
tla toconittacan	let us go and see	*déjanos ir y ver*
tonahualtezcauah	our enchanted mirror	*nuestro espejo encantado*
ac teotl	who is the god	*¿quién es el dios*
ac mahuiztli	who is the power	*quién es el poder*
ic tlapoztequi	who is messing up	*quién está fallando*
ic tlaxaxamania	who is shattering	*quién se está quebrando*
ic quixpoloa	who is undoing	*quién está deshaciendo*
in tochalchiuh	our jade	*nuestro jade*
in tocozqui	our jewel	*nuestras joyas*
in toquetzal?	our plume?	*nuestras plumas?*
tla xihualhuian	come on	*vengan*
tla toconotlecahuican	let us climb up	*déjanos subir*
tochalchiuhecahuaz	our jade ladder	*nuestra escalera de jade*
toMictlanhecahuaz	our Mictlan ladder	*nuestra escalera al Mictlan*
ahmo quin moztla	not tomorrow	*no hoy*
ahmo quin huiptla	or the day after	*ni mañana*
zan niman	but right now	*sino ahora mismo*
axcan toconittazque	we shall see	*veremos*
ac ye quimictia	who is killing	*quien está matando*
in teteoh impiltzin	the son of the gods	*al hijo de los dioses*
nomatca nehuatl	I myself	*yo mismo*
niTlamacazqui	I, Spirit in Flesh	*yo, Espíritu Encarnado*
niTlamantini	I, the Sage	*yo, el Sabio*
niNihmatcatictli	I, Lord of Mictlan:	*yo, el Señor de Mictlan:*
niMictlanTeuctli:		
quen ye quitlamachtia	will this cure him?	*¿lo curará esto?*
cuix quitlanahuitiz	will he get worse?	*¿se empeorará?*
ca cuix achicatiz?	will he last some time?	*¿durará algún tiempo?*

Itlahtlauhtiliz in tletl
Prayer to Fire
Oración al fuego
      Ruiz de Alarcón (V:2)

tla xihualhuian	come forth	*ven adelante*
nota	father of mine	*padre mío*
Nahui-Acatl Milintica	Four Reed Flaming	*Flameante Cuatro Junco*
Tzoncoztli	Yellow Hair	*Cabello Amarillo*
Tlahuizcalpan Teuctli	Lord of the House-of-Dawn	*Señor de la Casa-del-Amanecer*
Teteo Inta	Father of the Gods	*Padre de los Dioses*
Teteo Innan	Mother of the Gods	*Madre de los Dioses*
caoniquinhaulhuicac	I've brought forth	*he traído*
nonanhualteohuan	my enchanted gods	*mis dioses encantados*
noztacteohuan	my white gods	*mis dioses blancos*
tla xihualhuian	come forth	*vengan adelante*
Macuiltonaleque	five solar spirits each	*cada uno cinco espíritus solares*
tzoneptzitzinme	pearly-headed ones	*los de cabezas nacaradas*
in zan ce imithual	one-courtyard-owners	*dueños de-un-patio-real*
zan ce inchayahuacauh	bracket of a rail	*soportes de una vía*
tla toconittacan	let us look at	*déjanos ver*
tonalhualtezcauh, etc.	our enchanted mirror, etc.	*nuestro espejo encantado, etc.*
ca niman	right now	*ahora mismo*
aman	it shall be	*así será*
nomatca nehuatl	I myself	*yo mismo*
nOxomoco	I, Oxomoco	*yo, Oxomoco*
niCipactonal	I, Cipactonal	*yo, Cipactonal*
nicmati Huehueh	I, the Old Man's Friend	*yo, el amigo del Hombre Viejo*
nicmati Ilama	I, the Old Woman's Friend	*yo, el amigo de la Mujer Vieja*
niMictlanmati	I, Mictlan traveler	*yo, viajero Mictlan*
niTopanmati	I, Topan traveler	*yo, viajero Topan*
nomatca nehuatl	I myself	*yo mismo*
nitlamacazqui	I, Spirit in Flesh	*yo, Espíritu Encarnado*
niNahualteuctli	I, the Enchanter	*yo, el Encantador*

Tobacco
Tabaco
Piciyetl

piciete:	*piciete:*	*piciyetl:*
sacred dust	*polvo sagrado*	*teoteuhtli*
with lime:	*con cal:*	*tenextli piciyeyoh:*
tenexiete	*tenexiete*	*tenexyetl*
key	*medicina*	*tachcauh*
medicine	*clave*	*pahtli*
as smoke:	*como humo:*	*ipocyo:*
praising mist	*bruma venerada*	*ayahuitl tlachamahuani*
messenger	*mensajero*	*titlantli*
to heavens	*del cielo*	*ilhuicac yauh*
puffs	*soplos*	*quipitza*
blessings	*benditos*	*tlateochihualli*
the lips	*los labios*	*temac*
the hands	*las manos*	*tetenco*
the living	*las habitaciones*	*auh*
quarters	*del hogar*	*tecalpan*

El tal sortílego escoge de una mazorca y de entre mucho maíz los granos más asoma-
dos y hermosos, de los cuales entresaca tal vez diez y nueve granos, y esta diferencia
causa la que tienen en ponerlos sobre el lienzo en que se echa la suerte; escogidos los
dichos granos el tal sortílego les corta los picos con los dientes, luego tiende delante
de sí un lienzo doblado y bien extendido en manera que no haga arruga, luego pone
sobre él una parte de los granos según la cantidad que cogió.

El que escogió diez y nueve pone al lado derecho cuatro granos muy parejos, la
haz hacia arriba y las puntas hacia el lado izquierdo pone otros tantos con el mismo
orden y luego arroja otros cuatro sin orden enfrente de sí y queda con siete granos en
la mano; otros ponen cuatro en cada esquina y quedan nueve en la mano, que todos
hacen veinte y cinco; otros ponen en casa esquina siete y arrojan dos enfrente sin
orden y quedan con nueve en las mano, que todos hacen treinta y nueve . . .

Demandando las palabras del conjuro, arroja el maíz que tenía en la mano
en medio del lienzo, y según caen los maíces juzga la suerte. La regla que ordinario
tienen en juzgarla, es que si los maíces caen la faz hacia arriba, es buena suerte, v. gr.
Será buena la medicina sobre que se consulta, o parecerá la persona o cosa perdida
que se busca, y al contrario si los maíces caen la faz hacia abajo . . .

From his chosen ear of corn, the fortune teller selects nineteen or twenty-five
of the most outstanding and beautiful kernels, depending on his particular
method of divination. Then he bites off their nibs with his teeth and places
them before them on a cloth that has been stretched and smoothed so it con-
tains no wrinkles.

The one who has chosen nineteen puts forth very similar kernels on the
right side, with points facing and an equal number on the left side, with points
facing right. Then he randomly flings another four in front of him while hold-
ing the remaining seven in his hand. Those who use twenty-five kernels put
four in each corner and keep nine in the hand. Others put seven in each corner,
toss two in front, and keep nine in the hand, making thirty-nine in all . . .

Finally the seer pronounces the words of this spell while tossing the
kernels in his hand onto the middle of the cloth, and he determines the fortune
according to how they fall. The usual rule is that if the kernels fall face up, the
fortune is good—for example, the medicine upon which one has made consul-
tation will be good, or the person or thing one seeks will show up. The contrary
is true if the kernels fall face down . . .

Ruiz de Alarcón (V:3)

Achtopaihtolo ica centli
Divining with Corn
Adivinar con maíz
Ruiz de Alarcón (V:3)

tla xihualmohuica	welcome	*bienvenida*
Tlazopilli	Tlazopilli	*Tlazopilli*
Chicome-Coatl	Seven Snake	*Siete Serpiente*
tla xihualhuian	come forth	*vengan adelante*
Macuiltonaleque	five solar spirits each	*cada uno cinco espíritus solares*
cemithauleque	one-courtyard-owners	*dueños de-un-patio-real*
aman yequen eh	now at last	*finalmente ahora*
tla tiquittati	let us go see	*déjanos ir a ver*
in incamanal	their joke	*la broma de ellos*
in inetequipachol	his worry	*su preocupación*
cuix quin moztla?	will it be tomorrow?	*¿será mañana?*
cuix quin huiptla?	the day after?	*¿el día después?*
ca iman	right now	*ahora mismo*
aman	it shall be	*así será*
nomatca nehuatl	I myself	*yo mismo*
niCipactonal	I, Cipactonal	*yo, Cipactonal*
niHuehueh	I, the Ancient One	*yo, el Anciano*
ye itic nontlachiaz	soon I shall see	*pronto veré*
in namox	in my book	*en mi libro*
in notezcuah	in my mirror	*en mi espejo*
in tla quinamiqui pahtzintli	if this medicine cures him	*si esta medicina lo cura*
ahnozo motlanahuitia	or if he gets worse	*o si lo empeora*

Soul
Alma
Motonal

if you lose	*si pierdes*	***intla ticpolihui***
your tonal	*tu tonal*	***motonal***
might as well	*quizá*	***iuhqui***
be dead	*estés muerto*	***timiqui***

Tlaachtopaihtoliztli ittalli in atl
Divining by Looking in the Water
Adivinación mirando en el agua
Ruiz de Alarcón (VI:2)

The diviners who can read fate by looking in the water, Atlan Tlachixque, begin with the following incantation. When they hold the child over the water, if they see that the child's face is dark, as if covered by a shadow, they judge his future to be absent of fate and fortune. If the child's face appears bright in the water, they say he is not sick, or that the indisposition is very slight. In this case, they conclude he will get well without a cure, or they administer a treatment of incense. . . .

Los adivinos que pueden leer el destino por mirar en el agua, Atlan Tlachixque, comienzan con el siguiente conjuro. Cuando sostienen al niño sobre el agua, si ven que el rostro del niño es oscuro, como si estuviera ensombrecido, juzgan su futuro ausente de destino y fortuna. Si el rostro del niño aparece brillante en el agua, dicen que no está enfermo, o que la indisposición es leve. En este caso concluyen que se mejorará sin una cura, o le administren un tratamiento de incienso. . . .

tla cuel	come now!	*¡ven ahora!*
tla xihuallauh	come forth	*ven adelante*
noNan	Mother	*Madre*
Chalchiuhcueye	Chalchiuhcueye	*Chalchiuhcueye*
Chalchihuitl Icue	Jade-Skirted-One	*La de la Falda-de-Jade*
Chalchihuitl Ihuipil	Jade-Bloused-One	*La de la Blusa-de-Jade*
Xoxouhque Icue	Green-Skirted-One	*La de la Falda Verde*
Xoxouhque Ihuipil	Green-Bloused-One	*La de la Blusa Verde*
Iztac Cihuatl	White Woman	*Mujer Blanca*
tla toconittilican	let us look at	*déjanos ver*
in icnopiltzintli	this poor little child	*a este pobre niño*
azo oquicauh	perhaps his tonal	*tal vez su tonal*
itonaltzin	has left him	*lo ha dejado*

Wiser
Sabio
Nihmati

now I know	*ahora sé*	*ye nicmati*
why my father	*por qué mi padre*	*in tlein ic notah*
would go out	*iba afuera*	*quizaya*
and cry	*y lloraba*	*auh chocaya*
in the rain	*en la lluvia*	*quiyauhatlan*

Life in Motion
Vida en moción
Yoliliztli

something	*algo más*	*oc ye miec itlah*
more than nothing	*que nada*	*in ahmo ahtleh*
like morning	*como la mañana*	*iuhqui tlaztallotl*
sunlight or air	*luz solar o aire*	*auh ehecatl*
something	*algo alrededor*	*itlah itlan*
around a kiss	*de un beso*	*tennamiquiztli*
something	*algo en el interior*	*itlah ihtec*
within a flower	*de una flor*	*xochitl*
something light	*algo suave*	*itlah poyactic*
something sweet	*algo dulce*	*itlah tzopelic*
something deep	*algo hondo*	*itlah huehcatlan*
something free	*algo libre*	*itlah cactihcac*
something else	*algo más*	*itlah*
capable of turning	*capaz de volver*	*tetlanehueh*
caterpillars into	*a las orugas*	*in quipapalotilia*
butterflies	*mariposas*	*in payatl*

Messengers
Mensajeros
Titlantin

to / a / ipampa Victor di Suvero

chairs	sillas	ocoicpalli
doors	puertas	tlatzacuilli
walls	muros	caltechtli
leave	se	moquinquetzah
themselves	dejan	titlaniztli
messages	mensajes	netitlaniztli
down	abajo	intzintlan
above	arriba	imixco
everywhere	en todas partes	nohuiyan
murmurs	murmullos	ihcoyoquiztli
secrets	secretos	ichtacayotl
bits of	pedacitos de	cocotoctic
dreams	sueños	tetemic
to each	que dejan	quicamapachoah
other	entre sí	intlahtol

Flowers
Flores
Xochimeh

a day	*un día*	*cemilhuitica*
is all	*solo duramos*	*ahoquic*
we last	*una bocanada de aire*	*tinemih*
a breath!	*¡un aliento!*	*zan achihtzinca!*

We're One
Somos uno
Ticentlacah

sea	*mar*	*hueyi atl*
dust	*polvo*	*teuhtontli*
tear	*lágrimas*	*ixayotontli*
pollen	*polen*	*xinachtli*

6. HEALERS

CURANDEROS

IN TITICIH

Father

look, I have your pure cane

your fresh cane, you

my patron Mother

look how poor I am

how humble I am

poor woman am I

humble woman am I

tender woman, abundant woman am I

woman of big roots am I,

woman rooted below the water am I

woman who sprouts am I

woman like a begonia am I

I am going to the sky,

in your sight, before our glory

there my paper, my Book remains

woman who stops the world am I

legendary woman healer am I

my feelings are satisfied

because I carry your heart, I

because I carry your heart, Christ

because I carry your heart, Father

María Sabina (from a shamanic ceremony on the night of July 12, 1958, in Hautla de Jiménez, Oaxaca, Mexico)

Padre

mira, tengo tu caña pura

tu caña fresca, tú

mi patrón Madre

mira que tan pobre soy

que tan humilde soy

mujer pobre soy

mujer humilde soy

mujer tierna, mujer abundante soy

mujer de grandes raíces soy,

mujer enraizada abajo del agua soy

mujer que germina soy

mujer begonia soy

me estoy yendo al cielo,

a tu vista, antes de tu gloria

ahí mi papel, mi Libro queda

mujer que detiene al mundo soy

legendaria mujer sanadora soy

mi corazón está satisfecho

porque llevo tu corazón, yo

porque llevo tu corazón, Cristo

porque llevo tu corazón, Padre

María Sabina (de una ceremonia chamánica la noche del 12 de julio, 1958, en Huatla de Jiménez, Oaxaca, México)

Birth
Nacimiento
Tlacatiliztli

Cuaton	*Cuaton*	*in tiCuaton*
Caxxoch	*Caxxoch*	*in tiCaxxoch*
Goddesses	*Diosas*	*in ancihuateteoh*
of Love	*del Amor*	*in tlazohtlaliztli*
burst	*hagan explotar*	*tla xichichitotzacan*
the dam	*la presa*	*in yolihuani atl*
of life	*de la vida*	*tlatzauctli*
let the five	*dejen que los cinco*	*tla mocuepah*
solar spirits	*espíritus solares*	*in macuiltonalehqueh*
in each hand	*en cada mano*	*nenecoc amomac*
become a net	*se vuelvan red*	*in matlatl*
and catch	*y atrapen*	*inic ancahcizqueh*
this child	*a este niño*	*inin inconeuh*
of the gods	*de los dioses*	*in teteoh*

Reconciling
Reconciliación
Netetlazohtlaltilo
to / a / ipampa Lupe Macías

Chalchiuhcueye	*Chalchiuhcueye*	*Chalchiuhcueyeh*
Mother Water	*Madre Agua*	*Atlinan*
lakes, stars	*lagos, estrellas*	*in atezcatl, in cicitlalin*
snakes and all:	*serpientes y todo:*	*in cocoah, in ye mochi:*
everyone is your cuate	*cada uno es tu cuate*	*in mochintin mocoauh*
a mirror to yourself:	*un espejo de ti misma:*	*motezcauh tehhuatl:*
break up the illusion	*rompe la ilusión*	*xixamani in teixcuepaliztli*
take off the mask	*quítate la máscara*	*xiquicohcopina in moxayac*
you are naked	*estás desnuda*	*tipetlauhtoc*
you are stripped	*estás despojada*	*tixipehua*
you are bone	*eres hueso*	*tomiyoti*
you are dust	*eres polvo*	*titeuhti*
don't look back	*no mires atrás*	*macamo xitlaitta micampa*
look within:	*mira dentro:*	*ma ximotta motech:*
accept the woman	*acepta la mujer*	*ma xiccui in cihuatl*
the spirit is female	*el espíritu es hembra*	*cihuatic ca teyoliya*
read the silence	*lee el silencio*	*xicopohua in cactimaniliztli*
enter the silence	*entra en el silencio*	*xicalqui itech cactimaniliztli*
smell the fire	*huele el fuego*	*xiquihnecui in tletl*
of each morning	*de cada mañana*	*oc yoyohuac*
honor the dirt	*honra la tierra*	*xiquimahuiztla*
in your fingernails	*en tus uñas*	*in mozti itlallo*
restore the balance	*restablece el balance*	*xiquipahti moNan*
of your Mother	*de tu Madre*	*itlatecpanaliz*
water of one ocean	*agua de un océano*	*tiatl in icel apan*
flower of the Sun	*flor del Sol*	*tixochitl in Tonatiuh*
walking calendar:	*calendario itinerante:*	*titonalamatl in tinehnenqui:*
don't shame yourself!	*¡no te avergüences de ti misma!*	*macamo xipinahua*

Face and Heart
Cara y corazón
In ixtli in yollotl

to / a / ipampa J. P.

may our ears	que nuestros oídos	ma quicacqui
hear	escuchen	tonacaz in
what nobody	lo que nadie	ayac quinequi
wants to hear	quiere escuchar	quicacquiz
may our eyes	que nuestros ojos	ma quitta
see	vean	tix in
what everyone	lo que todos	mochin quinequi
wants to hide	quieren esconder	quinayaz
may our mouths	que nuestras bocas	ma quihtoa
speak	hablen	tocan in
our true faces	nuestras verdaderas caras	nelli tix ihuan
and hearts	y corazones	toyolloh
may our arms	que nuestros brazos	ma cuauhuiti
be branches	sean ramas	toma in
that give shade	que den sombra	quitemaca
and joy	y alegría	iehcauhyo, tepac
let us be drizzle	déjanos ser llovizna	ma tayahuitican
a sudden storm	una tormenta repentina	ma tapachihuacan
let us get wet	déjanos empaparnos	ma titociyahuacan
in the rain	en la lluvia	quiyappan
let us be the key	déjanos ser la llave	ma titocuepacan
the hand the door	la mano la puerta	in tlatlapoloni in maitl
the kick the ball	la patada la pelota	in tlatzacuilli in tlateliczaliztli
the road	el camino	in olloli in ohtli
let us arrive	déjanos llegar	ma tihualahcican
as children	como niños	iuhqueh pipltin
to this huge	a este inmenso	in hueyi
playground:	lugar de juegos:	ahuilpan:
the universe	el universo	in cemanahuactli

En esto le hice [Domingo Hernández] poner en buen recaudo, y antes de pasar un día de su prisión se juntó gran número de indios, que trayéndome un presente, me pidieron muy encarecidamente le soltase, porque era su remedio y consuelo y de todas sus enfermedades. . . .

I had [Domingo Hernández] placed under good custody. Before he had spent a day in prison, a great number of Indians gathered. They bought me presents and begged very earnestly that I set him free because he was the remedy and consolation for all their illnesses. . . .

Ruiz de Alarcón (VI:19)

Domingo Hernández

please	*por favor*	*tla*
let him free	*libéralo*	*xiquimaquixti*
he's kind	*es noble*	*yehhuatl huelnezqui*
our remedy	*es nuestro remedio*	*tonamic*
he's crossed	*ha cruzado*	*oquimauh*
the Nine Rooms	*las Nueve Habitaciones*	*in chiucnauhcan*
he cures	*él cura*	*tlapalehuia*
he heals	*él sana*	*tepahtia*
with atlinan	*con atlinan*	*atlinan ica*
water mother	*madre agua*	*atl ichipinca*
with yauhtli	*con yauhtli*	*yauhtli ica*
sweet marigolds	*cempasúchiles*	*cempohualxochitl*
let him	*deja*	*ma quitzonquixti*
finish his wind:	*que termine su viento:*	*iehecatzin:*
"in Xoxohuix Tlamacazqui	*"in Xoxohuix Tlamacazqui*	*"in Xoxohuix Tlamacazqui*
in Yayahuic	*in Yayahuic*	*in Yayahuic*
Tlamacazqui	*Tlamacazqui*	*Tlamancazqui*
(Green Spirit	*(Espíritu Verde*	*(xopan ehecatl*
Dark Spirit)	*Espíritu Oscuro)*	*yohualli ehecatl)*
in Nomie Patris	*in Nomine Patris*	*ica in itocatzin tetatzin*
et Filli	*et Filli*	*ihuan tepiltzin*
et Spiritus Sancti"	*et Spiritus Sancti"*	*ihuan Espíritu Santo"*

Herbs
Hierbas
In pahtli

in the market	*en el mercado*	*tiyanquizco*
herbs begin	*las hierbas comienzan*	*in pahtli*
to sing	*a cantar*	*quehua*
a song	*una canción*	*icuic*
of small leaves	*de hojas pequeñas*	*in ahtlapaltzintli*
of green thumbs	*de manos verdes*	*in mahpilli in milchihua*
ground herbs	*hierbas de tierra*	*tlalpahtli*
water herbs	*hierbas de agua*	*apahtli*
sky herbs	*hierbas del cielo*	*ilhuicapahtli*
herbs for	*hierbas por*	*pahtli in quipahti*
all pains	*todos los dolores*	*in cococ*
and afflictions	*y aflicciones*	*in teohpouhqui*
the root	*la raíz*	*inelhuayo*
of coanenepilli	*de coanenepilli*	*coanenepilli*
for sunstroke	*para la insolación*	*ica ahmo tonalhuiteco*
drops	*gotas*	*tenextli*
of tenexiete	*de tenexiete*	*ichipinca*
for earaches	*para el dolor de oído*	*ica ahmo nacazcualo*
for swollen heads	*para la cabeza inflamada*	*inelhuayo*
the root	*la raíz*	*chalalahtli quicehuia*
of chalalatli	*de chalalatli*	*in tzonteconcocolli*
mesquite sap	*la savia del mezquite*	*in mizquicopalli*
for curing	*para sanar*	*tlacuihcuilia*
the eyes	*los ojos*	*teix*
toothaches gone	*el dolor de diente*	*tetlanatonahuiliz*
with copal	*se va con copal*	*mopahtia copaltica*
and piciete	*y piciete*	*piciyetica*

teas	tés	xiuhatl
oils	aceites	chiyahuallotl
incenses	inciensos	popochtli
sore throats	garganta inflamada	tozcamiyahuacihuiliztli
chest pains	dolor del pecho	elchiquiuhcocoliztli
bye bye	adiós adiós	pohpolihui
I put	pongo	nocxi cihuaya
my wet feet	mis pies mojados	niquiquetza
on heated stones	en piedras calientes	ipan totonqui tetl
and start	y comienzo	nipehua
walking	a caminar	in nehnemi
barefoot	descalzo	mocactotonqui
over and over	una y otra vez	ic cem mochipa
my own	sobre mi	niquihicza
back bones	columna vertebral	nocuitlapanomiyo

Ipampa telpan cococ
For Strained Chests
Para los pechos cansados
Ruiz de Alarcón (VI:14)

This affliction comes from working too much with the arms and is frequently seen in those who dig in the mines. To remedy a strained chest, piciete (crushed tobacco) and yauhtli (anise) are applied along with this spell.

Esta aflicción se produce por trabajar mucho con los brazos, y es frecuentemente vista en aquellos que cavan en las minas. Para remediar un pecho cansado, piciete (tabaco machucado) y yauhtli (anise) son aplicados junto con este conjuro:

tla xihuallauh	come	*ven*
Chiucnauhtlatetzotzon	Nine-Times-Powdered-One	*Nueve-Veces-Empolvado*
Chiucnauhtlatecanpani	Nine-Times-Crushed-One	*Nueve-Veces-Pulverizado*
yayauhqui coacihuiztli	dark pain	*dolor oscuro*
xoxouhqui coacihuiztli	green pain:	*dolor verde:*
ac tlacatl	who is the person	*¿quién es la persona?*
ac mahuiztli	who is the power	*¿quién es el poder?*
in ye quixpoloa	who is hurting	*¿quién está lastimando*
nomacehual	my fellow human?	*a mi compañero humano?*
tla xictotoca	chase it away	*corretéalo*
tla xihuian	go to it	*ve a éste*
tlazotli	precious ones	*preciosos unos*
campa in omotecato	where does it lie?	*¿dónde se encuentra?*
[text missing]	in my enchanted rib cage?	*¿en mi caja torácica encantada?*
	in my enchanted backbone?	*¿en mi columna vertebral?*
itic in nonahualtzontecomatl	to my enchanted head	*a mi cabeza encantada*
tictocaticalaquiz	go swiftly	*ve prontamente*
tlamacazque	you, spirits	*ustedes espíritus*
Macuiltonaleque	five solar spirits each	*cada uno cinco espíritus solares*
ma ammopinauhtitin	do your duty	*cumple con tu deber*
Cozauhqui Cihuatl	you, Yellow Woman	*tú, Mujer Amarilla*

Madre
Mother
Tonantzin

Madre	Mother	*Tonantzin*
¿aquí estás	are you here	*cuix ticah*
con nosotros?	with us?	*totloc?*
enjuáganos	wipe up	*tla xiquipohpohua*
el sudor	our sweat	*tixayo*
las lágrimas	our tears	*titonal*
Coatlicue	Coatlicue	*Coatlicue*
tú que reinas	you who rule	*ipan titlahtoa*
sobre las serpientes	over snakes	*in cocoah*
Chalchiuhcueye	Chalchiuhcueye	*Chalchiuhcueyeh*
haznos	grant us	*tla xiquimocahuili*
el favor	our request	*totlaitlaniliz*
Citlalcueye	Citlalcueye	*Citlalcueyeh*
que nos guíen	let your stars	*ma techyacanilia*
tus estrellas	guide us	*mocitlal*
Guadalupe	Guadalupe	*Guadalupe*
sé nuestra aurora	be our dawn	*xiye totlahuizcal*
nuestra esperanza	our hope	*xiye tonetemachil*
¡bandera	the flag	*xiye ipan*
y fuego de	and fire of	*ihuan itleuh*
nuestra rebelión!	our rebellion!	*totzonteyo!*

Snake Woman

La Llorona
Cihuacoatl

in the barrios	*en los barrios*	*cahcalpolco*
La Llorona	*a La Llorona*	*poliuhtiuh*
has run out	*se le acabaron*	*ichoquiz*
of tears	*las lágrimas*	**in Zohuaehecatl**

Ipampa nepoztequiliztli
For Bone Fractures
Para fracturas de hueso
Ruiz de Alarcón (VI:22)

tle oax nohuetiuh	what have my elder sisters—	*¿Qué han hecho mis hermanas*
in Chicuetecpacihuatl	Eight Flint Woman and	*mayores—Mujer Ocho Pedernal*
Tlaloccihuatl	Tlaloc Woman—done?	*y Mujer Tlaloc?*
omonapaloque	they've embraced	*han abrazado*
omonacochoque	they've reduced	*han reducido*
teteo impiltzin	the child of the gods	*el hijo de los dioses*
ca nehuatl	but I am	*pero yo soy*
nitlamacazqui	the Spirit in Flesh	*el Espíritu Encarnado*
niQuetzalcoatl	Quetzalcoatl	*Quetzalcoatl*
niyani Mictlan	I've gone to Mictlan	*he ido a Mictlan*
niyani Topan	I've gone to Topan	*he ido a Topan*
niyani ChiucnauhMictlan	I've gone to Nine Mictlan	*he ido a Nueve Mictlan*
ompa niccuiz	there I will get	*allá obtendré*
in Mictlanomitl	the Mictlan bone	*el hueso Mictlan*
otlalacoque	they've messed up—	*han confundido—*
in tlamacazque	the spirits	*a los espíritus*
in teuhtotome	the dust-birds	*a las aves-de-polvo*
otlaxaxamanique	something they shattered	*algo que han estrellado*
otlapoztecque	something they broke	*algo que han roto*
auh in axcan	but now we shall glue it	*pero ahora tendremos que*
ticzazalozque	back together	*pegarlo de nuevo*
ticpatizque	we shall heal it	*lo curaremos*
tla cuel	come now	*ahora ven*
nomazacoamecatzin	my deersnake rope	*mi cuerda de serpiente-venado*
tla nican xontlapixto	go stand watch here	*levántate y vigila aquí*
ma nen tontlatlaco	beware of messing up—	*ten cuidado de regarla—*
mopan necoz in moztla	I'll see you tomorrow	*mañana te veo*

Massage
Masaje
Nepahpacholiztli

hands put	*las manos ponen*	*tema*
our pains	*nuestros dolores*	*quicochitia*
to sleep	*a dormir*	*tocococatzin*
lead them	*guíalos*	*quiyacanilia*
as fish to	*como peces a*	*iuhqui michin*
whirlpools	*los remolinos*	*itec axictli*

Tetzotzopitzaliztli ipampa in tetepotz
Acupuncture for the Back
Acupuntura para la espalda
Ruiz de Alarcón (VI:23)

tla cuel!	come now!	*¡ahora ven!*
xoxohuic coatl	green snake	*serpiente verde*
cozahuic coatl	yellow snake	*serpiente amarilla*
tlatlahuic coatl	red snake	*serpiente roja*
iztac coatl	white snake	*serpiente blanca*
ye huitz	soon will come	*pronto vendrá*
iztac cuautlatzotzopitzqui	the white eagle puncturer	*la pinchadora águila blanca*
nohuiyan nemiz	she will be everywhere—	*estará en todas partes—*
intetl itic	inside the rocks	*dentro de las rocas*
in cuahuitli itic	inside the trees	*dentro de los árboles*
auh in ac in ipan aciz	whatever she finds	*lo que encuentre*
quicuaz	she will eat	*comerá*
quipopoloz	she will destroy	*destruirá*

Ihuicpa in totonqui
For Fevers
Para la fiebre
Ruiz de Alarcón (VI:29)

For fevers the Indians use remedies of ololiuhqui, peyote, atlinan ("water mother") or other herbs. The method is to grind the herb, dissolve it in cold water, then administer it as an enema with the following spell and incantation.

Para la fiebre los indios usan remedios de ololiuhqui, peyote, atlinan ("agua madre") u otras hierbas. El método es el de moler la hierba, disolverla en agua fría, después administrar con un enema con el siguiente hechizo y conjuro.

tla cuel!	come on!	*¡adelante!*
tla xihuallauh	come now	*ven ahora*
Xoxouhqui Cihuatl	Green Woman	*Mujer Verde*
tlaxicpehuiti	take away	*llévate*
xoxouhqui totonqui	the green heat	*el calor verde*
yayauhqui totonqui	the dark heat	*el calor oscuro*
tlatlauhqui totonqui	the red heat	*el calor rojo*
cozauhqui totonqui	the yellow heat	*el calor amarillo*
ye onca nimitztitlan	now I send you there	*ahora te envío allá*
Chicomoztoc	to the Seven Caves	*a las Siete Cavernas*
ahmo quin moztla	not tomorrow	*no mañana*
ahmo quin hiptla	or the day after	*o el día después*
niman axcan	but right now	*sino ahora*
ticquixtiz	you shall banish this	*tú harás desaparecer esto*
ac teotl	who is the god	*¿quién es el dios?*
ac mahuiztli	who is the power	*¿quién es el poder?*
in ye quixpoloa	who is destroying	*¿quién está destruyendo*
motlachihualtzin	your creation?	*tu creación?*
nomatca nehuatl	I myself	*yo mismo*
niNahualteuctli	I, the Enchanter	*yo, el Encantador*

Ihuicpa in ciyahuiztli auh in coacihuiztli
For Fatigue and Body Pains
Para la fatigua y los dolores de cuerpo
Ruiz de Alarcón (VI:31)

For fatigue, which the Indians call *cuacuauhtiliztli* ("stiffness"), and for body pains, the method of treatment is to cause an evacuation by adminstering an enema or clyster. The one who practices this cure heats the soles of the feet and the heels, something which they call *ytetleiza* ("fire-treading"), and massages the body from the kidneys and loins to the ankles while adding this spell:

Para la fatiga, la que los indios llaman cuacuauhtiliztli *("rigidez"), y para los dolores de cuerpo, el método de tratamiento es causar una evacuación al adminstrar un enema o clyster. Quien practica esta cura calienta las plantas de los pies y los talones, algo que ellos llaman* ytetleiza *("caminar en el fuego"), y masajea el cuerpo desde los riñones y las ingles a los tobillos mientras agrega este conjuro:*

tla xihuallauh	come here	*ven aquí*
cozahuic neahanalli	yellow relaxer	*relajante amarillo*
xoxouhqui neahanalli	green relaxer:	*relajante verde:*
nican tictemozque	here we shall seek out	*aquí buscaremos*
in cozauhqui cuacuauhtiliztli	the yellow stiffness	*la rigidez amarilla*
xoxouhqui cuacuauhtiliztli	the green stiffness	*la rigidez verde*

Magdalena Petronila Xochiquetzal, an old blind woman from Huitzoco, used to practice this fraud. Another woman called Justina from the same village used to employ the herb that they call *tzopilotl*, also applied as an enema, with this next spell:

Magdalena Petronila Xochiquetzal, una mujer anciana ciega de Huitzoco, solía practicar este fraude. Otra mujer llamada Justina, de la misma villa, solía emplear la hierba que llaman tzopilotl *también aplicada en un enema, con este conjuro:*

tla xihuallauh	come here	*ven aquí*
Iztac-Cihuatl	White Woman:	*Mujer Blanca:*
tla xoxompopoloti	go and destroy	*ve y destruye*
in xoxouhqui coacihuiztli	the green pain	*el dolor verde*
yayahuic coacihuiztli	the dark pain	*el dolor oscuro*
(quitoznequi cuacuauhtiliztli)	(meaning the stiffness)	*(refiriéndose a la rigidez)*

Note

At this point, it seems to me that I should speak of something that should be of interest to any person whose charge is the governance and customs of these natives, something so rooted and accepted among them, and so harmful that the Enemy (who is vigilant for our detriment) has introduced, taking advantage of their natural weakness and inclination.

This is that at the same time that they are compelled to personal service, in farm work as well as in the mines, where they usually experience so much damage to their bodily health from excessive work—labor which borne out of love for God would be of much spiritual benefit— but the Devil has established his league against it by persuading them that, if they get drunk to excess before going to work, they will gather such strength and vigor that they would easily be able to bear such tasks, and following that, to recover their strength lost in drunkenness. They call these harmful drunken sprees *necehualiztli* ("refreshing oneself").

Thus, with their drinking and the intolerable work that they have, they end up getting sick and dying, without taking warning from the continual deaths that come about each day from these drunken sprees. For this reason, the ministers and curates ought to try to convince them of the serious harm that comes to their bodies and souls from this. The same goes for the secular authorities: *in virga ferrea* ("with a rod of iron"), since experience shows that no gentle means is of use in extirpating this infernal vice, at the hands of which such a great multitude is dying. This miserable generation is entirely destroying and consuming itself, taking death in their hands.

Nota

En este punto, me parece que debo hablar de algo que debe ser de interés para cualquier persona cuyo cargo es el gobernar y las costumbres de estos nativos, algo tan enraizado y aceptado entre ellos, y tan dañino que el Enemigo (quien es vigilante para nuestro detrimento) ha introducido, para aprovecharse de su debilidad natural e inclinación.

Esto es, que al mismo tiempo sientan un llamado al servicio personal, en trabajo de campo así como en las minas, donde usualmente experimentan tanto daño a su salud corporal por el trabajo excesivo— labor que motivada por el amor a Dios sería de mucho beneficio espiritual—pero el Diablo ha establecido su liga contra esto al persuadirlos de que si se emborrachan en exceso antes de ir a trabajar, juntarán tal fuerza y vigor que ellos fácilmente serán capaces de soportar tales tareas, y siguiendo eso, recobrar su fuerza perdida en la ebriedad. Llaman a esto juerga dañina de ebriedad necehualiztli *("refrescándose a uno mismo").*

Entonces, con su tendencia a la bebida y el trabajo intolerable que tienen, terminan enfermándose y mueren, sin tomar en cuenta la advertencia de las muertes continuas a las que se enfrentan cada día como resultado de estas juergas embriagantes. Por esta razón los ministros y curadores deben tratar de convencerlos del daño serio que llega a sus cuerpos y almas por esto. Lo mismo aplica a las autoridades seculares: in virga ferrea *("con una barra de hierro"), ya que la experiencia muestra que ningún medio suave es de uso para extirpar este vicio infernal por el cual tan grande multitud está muriendo. Esta generación miserable se está completamente destruyendo y consumiendo así misma, tomando a la muerte en sus manos.*

Holocaust
Holocausto
Mixtlatihtoqueh

your eyes	*tus ojos*	*mix*
don't see	*no ven*	*ahmo teitta*
your ears	*tus oídos*	*monacaz*
are plugged	*están tapados*	*ahmo tlacaqui*
this hell's	*este infierno es*	*inin mictlan*
your invitation	*tu invitación*	*motlachihual*
we're morning	*somos flores*	*titlahuizcalxochitih*
flowers cut	*cortadas en la mañana*	*titotequih*
bleeding in	*que sangran en*	*tezquizah*
your altar	*tu altar*	*momomozco*
vases	*vasijas*	*moxicalco*
fields mines	*campos minas*	*momilpan motlapehualtec*

Working Hand
Manos trabajadoras
Noma tlaayini

we clean	*limpiamos*	*tiquipopohuah*
your room	*tu habitación*	*mocochiyan*
we do	*lavamos*	*tiquipahpacah*
your dishes	*tus platos*	*mocax*
a footnote	*un pie de página*	*ca zaniyoh*
for you	*para ti*	*timomacehualhuan*
but hands	*pero manos*	*auh tema*
like these	*como éstas*	*iuhqui inin*
one day	*un día*	*quemmaniyan*
will write	*escribirán*	*quihcuiloah*
the main text	*el texto principal*	*in achtic amoxtli*
of this land	*de esta tierra*	*in nican tlalli ipan*

Not Poems
No poemas
Ahmo xochicuicatl

just ink	*sólo tinta*	*zan tlilatl*
on paper	*en papel*	*icpac amatl*
like air	*como aire*	*iuhqui ehecatl*
like you	*como tú*	*iuhqui tehhuatl*

Itlaquetzal Yappan
The Story of Yappan
El cuento de Yappan
Ruiz de Alarcón (VI:32)

In the first era, when those that now are animals were humans, there was one whose name was Yappan. For the sake of improving his condition in the transmutation that he felt was near, in order to placate the gods and capture their benevolence, he went off alone to do penance in abstinence and chastity. He lived on a rock called Tehuehuetl ("Stone-Drum"). Because Yappan persevered in his intentions they placed someone called Yaotl ("the Warrior") to watch him.

During this time, Yappan was tempted by some women but not overcome. Meanwhile the two sister goddesses, Citlalcueye and Chachiuhcueye (who are the Milky Way and Water), foresaw that Yappan was going to be turned into a scorpion and that, if he persisted in his purpose, after being turned into a scorpion, he would kill all those he stung. Seeking a remedy for this bad scenario, they decided that their sister, the goddess Xochiquetzal, should go down to tempt Yappan. She descended to where Yappan was and said to him:

En la primera era cuando esos que ahora son animales eran humanos, había uno cuyo nombre era Yappan. Por el bien de mejorar su condición en la transmutación que dejó cerca, para aplacar a los dioses y gozar de su benevolencia, fue solo a hacer penitencia en abstinencia y castidad. Vivió en una roca llamada Tehuehuetl ("Piedra-Tambor"). Porque Yappan perseveró en sus intenciones pusieron a alguien llamado Yaotl ("el Guerrero") para vigilarlo.

Durante este tiempo, Yappan fue tentado por algunas mujeres pero no lograron vencerlo. Mientras tanto las dos hermanas diosas, Citlalcueye y Chalchiuhcueye (quienes son la Vía Láctea y el Agua), predijeron que Yappan iba a ser convertido en escorpión y que, si persistía en su propósito, después de haber sido transformado en un escorpión, el mataría a todos a los que picara. Al buscar un remedio para este mal escenario, ellas decidieron que su hermana, la diosa Xochiquetzal, debía bajar para tentar a Yappan. Ella bajó hasta donde estaba Yappan y le dijo:

Xochiquetzal:	Xochiquetzal:	*Xochiquetzal:*
"noquichtiuh	"dear brother	*"querido hermano*
Yappan	Yappan	*Yappan*
onihualla	I am here	*estoy aquí*

| 132 |

nimohueltiuh	I, your elder sister	*yo, tu hermana mayor*
niXochiquetzal	Xochiquetzal,	*Xochiquetzal,*
nimiztlapalaco	have come to greet you	*he venido a saludarte*
nimizciauhquetzaco"	I've come to meet you"	*he venido a conocerte"*

Yappan:	Yappan:	Yappan:
"otihuallauh	"welcome	*"bienvenida*
nohueltiuhe	dear sister	*querida hermana*
Xochiquetzal"	Xochiquetzal"	*Xochiquetzal"*

Xochiquetzal:	Xochiquetzal:	Xochiquetzal:
"onihualla	"I am down here	*"estoy aquí abajo*
campa ye nitlecoz"	where can I climb up?"	*¿dónde puedo subir?"*

Yappan:	Yappan:	Yappan:
"xicchie	"wait	*"espera*
ye ompa niyauh"	I'm going down for you"	*bajo por ti"*

At that, the goddess Xochiquetzal climbed up and, covering him with her huipil ("blouse"), he failed in his purpose (of chastity). The cause of this fall was that Xochiquetzal was a stranger and a goddess who came from the heavens, which they call *chicnauhtopan*, which means "from the nine places." With this, the spy, Yaotl, who had not fallen asleep, said to Yappan:

Con esto la diosa Xochiquetzal subió y lo cubrió con su huipil ("blusa"), el falló su propósito (de castidad). La cause de este fallo fue que Xochiquetzal era una extraña y una diosa que vino de los cielos que él llamó chicnauhtopan, *que significa "de los nueve lugares." Con esto, el espia, Yaotl, que no se había quedado dormido, dijo a Yappan:*

Yaotl:	Yaotl:	Yaotl:
"ahmo tipinahua	"aren't you ashamed	*"¿no estás avergonzado*
tlamacazqui Yappan	priest Yappan	*sacerdote Yappan*
otitlatlaco	for messing up?	*por haber fracasado?*
"in quexquich cahuitl	"however long	*"por tanto como*
tlimonemitiz in tlalticpac	you live on earth	*vivas en la tierra*
"ahmo tla huel in tlaltipac	"you shall do nothing well	*"no harás nada bien*
ahmo tle huel tictequipanoz	you shall achieve nothing	*no lograrás nada*

"mitztocayotizque	"common folks	*"gente común*
in macehualtin 'tiColotl'	will call you 'Scorpion'	*te llamará 'Escorpión'*
"ca nican nimitztocayotia	"for here I call you	*"aquí te llamo*
nimitzicamati 'tiColotl'	I name you 'Scorpion'	*te nombro 'Escorpión'*
"xihualhuian	"come forth	*"ven adelante*
iuhque tiyez"	for you shall be this way"	*serás de esta manera"*
Tlahtlaquetzqui:	Narrator:	*Narrador:*
"oquiquechcoton	"he beheaded him	*"lo decapitó*
oquiquechpanoh	he carried on his shoulders	*llevó en hombros*
itzontecon	his head	*su cabeza*
"yehuatl ica itoca	"because of this he is	*"por esto él es llamado*
'Tzonteconmama'"	called 'Head Carrier'"	*'El Cargador de Cabeza'"*

After being beheaded, Yappan was immediately transformed into a scorpion, and Yaotl went after Yappan's wife, cut off her head and transformed her into a scorpion. She was called Tlahuitzin ("Red-Ochre"). And since Yappan had sinned, the goddess Citlalcueye decided that not all who were stung by a scorpion would die. And Yaotl was changed into a locust, which they call Ahuaca Chapullin ("Avocado-Locust") or Tzonteconmamama ("Head-Carrier").

Después de haber sido decapitado, Yappan fue inmediatamente transformado en un escorpión, y Yaotl fue tras la esposa de Yappan, cortó su cabeza y la transformó en escorpión. Ella fue llamada Tlahitzin ("Rojo-Ocre"). Y como Yappan había pecado, la diosa Citlalcueye decidió que no todos los que fueran picados por un escorpión morirían. Y Yaotl fue transformado en un chapulín, al que llamaron Ahuaca Chapullin ("Aguacate Chapullín") o Tzonteconmamama ("Cargador-de-Cabeza").

Ihuicpa itlaminal ihuan iztlac in colotl
Against Scorpion's Sting and Poison
Contra la picadura y veneno del escorpión
Ruiz de Alarcón (VI:31)

nomatca nehuatl	I myself	*yo mismo*
niTlamacazqui	I, priest	*yo, sacerdote*
Chicome-Xochitl	Seven Flower	*Siete Flor*
tla xihualhuian	come forth	*ven adelante*
Tlamacazqui Yappan	priest Yappan	*sacerdote Yappan*
Huitzcol	Curved Thorn	*Espina Curveada*
tle ica in teca timocacayahua?	why do you mock people?	*¿Por qué te burlas de la gente?*
cuix ahmo ye ticmati	don't you know by now?	*¿No sabes ahora?*
ahmo ye moyollo quimati	don't you know in your heart	*¿No sabes en tu corazón*
in omitznezahualpoztequito	she went to break your fast	*que fue a romper tu ayuno*
nohueltiuh	—my elder sister	*—mi hermana mayor*
Xochiquetzal	Xochiquetzal—	*Xochiquetzal—*
in ompa Tehuehueticpac	there on top of Stone Drum	*allá en la cima de la Piedra Tambor?*
in ompa in ica	there where you	*¿allá donde tú*
otimocacayauh?	mocked her?	*te burlaste de ella?*
ahmo tle in huel ticchihuaz	there's nothing you can do	*no hay nada que puedas hacer*
ahmo tle in huel tictequipanoz	there's nothing you can cause	*no hay nada que puedas causar*
nepa huecca	make fun of people	*búrlate de la gente*
teca ximocacayahuati	far away from here	*lejos de aquí*
nepa hueca	amuse yourself with people	*diviértete con la gente*
teca ximahuiltiti	far away from here	*lejos de aquí*
tla xihualhuian	come forth	*ven adelante*
nonan Tlalteuctli	Tlalteuctli, Mother Earth	*Tlalteuctli, Madre Tierra*
zan ihuiyan xictlacahuati	calm down quietly	*calma calladamente*
in Tlamacazqui Yappan	the priest Yappan	*al sacerdote Yappan*
Pelxayaque	the Bare Mask	*la Máscara Vacía*

ma zan ihuiyan quiza	let him leave quietly	*déjalo salir calladamente*
ma zan ihuiyan mitzlacahui	let him depart unnoticed	*déjalo irse sin que se note*
cuix quin moztla	will he go tomorrow	*¿irá mañana*
cuix quin huiptla yaz?	or the day after?	*o el día después?*
ca niman	right now	*ahora mismo*
aman	it shall be	*así será*
in tlacamo quizaz	if he doesn't leave	*si no sale*
in tlacamo yaz	if he doesn't go	*si no se va*
ca oc nehuatl nicmati	I will know	*lo sabré*
in tleh ipan nicchihuaz	what to do about it!	*¡qué hacer de esto!*

If the venom has already taken possession of the patient, the conjurer invokes Xochiquetzal by saying:

Si el veneno ha tomado posesión del paciente, el conjurador invoca a Xochiquetzal al decir:

noquichtiuh Pelxayaque	brother Bare Mask	*hermano Máscara Vacía*
ahmo tipinahua?	aren't you ashamed?	*¿no tienes vergüenza?*
tleh ica teca timocacayahua?	why do you make fun of people?	*¿por qué te burlas de la gente?*
tle ica in teca timahuitltia?	why do you amuse yourself with people?	*¿por qué te diviertes con la gente?*
cuix ahmo ye ticmati	don't you know by now	*¿no sabes para ahora?*
ahmo quimattica in moyollo	don't you know in your heart	*¿no sabes en tu corazón?*
in onimitznezahualpoztequito	I went to break your fast	*que fui a romper tu ayuno*
in ompa Tehuehueticpac	there on top of Stone Drum	*allá en la cima de la Piedra Tambor*
in niXochiquetzal	I, Xochiquetzal—	*yo, Xochiquetzal—*
in ompa nohuan oticoch	there where you slept with me?	*allá donde dormiste conmigo?*
onihualla	I am here	*estoy aquí*
in nimohueltituh	I, your elder sister	*yo, tu hermana mayor*
niXochiquetzal	I, Xochiquetzal	*yo, Xochiquetzal*

nimitzlapaloco	I've come to greet you	*he venido a saludarte*
mimitzciauhquetzaco	I've come to meet you	*he venido a conocerte*
za ihuiyan xictlacahui	just leave alone	*solo deja en paz*
in nomacehual	my fellow human	*a mi compañero humano*
tla nimitzhuipiltepoya	let my protect you with my huipil	*déjame protegerte con mi huipil*
tla nimitzhipllapacho	let me cover you with my huipil	*déjame envolverte con mi huipil*
tla nimitzhuipilquilmilo	let me wrap you with my huipil	*déjame cubrirte con mi huipil*
za ihuiyan xicochi	just sleep quietly	*solo duerme calladamente*
tla nimitzmacochihui	let me embrace you	*déjame abrazarte*
tla nimitznapalo	let me take you in my arms	*déjame llevarte en mis brazos*
tla nimitznahuatequi	let me kiss you	*déjame besarte*

If the conjurer is a man, he covers the sick person with a blanket, embracing and caressing him. If the healer is a woman, she does likewise with her huipil, and also takes a ribbon or small cord from her hair and ties off the wounded limb or the sick person saying:

Si el conjurador es hombre, cubre a la persona enferma con una manta, lo abraza y acaricia. Si la curandera es mujer, hace lo mismo con el huipil, y también lleva un listón o cordón pequeño de su pelo y lo amarra al miembro lastimado de la persona enferma, dice:

noquichtiuh	elder brother aren't you	*hermano mayor*
ahmo tipanahua	ashamed	*¿no estás avergonzado*
titeelehuia?	of hurting people?	*de lastimar a la gente?*
iuhqui tiyez in	you shall be like this . . .	*serás así . . .*

[Here the conjurer draws a symbol which Ruiz de Alarcón had painted in the margin of his original text; this symbol is unfortunately now missing in the extant copy of the *Tratado*.]

[*Aquí el conjurador dibuja un símbolo que Ruiz de Alarcón ha pintado en el margen de su texto original; este símbolo ahora está desafortunadamente perdido en la copia restante del Tratado.*]

iuhqui tiyez in   you shall be like this . . .   *tú serás así . . .*

[the missing symbol is repeated]

[*el símbolo perdido es repetido*]

nican nimitzilpico   here I've come to tie you up   *he venido aquí para amarrarte*
nimitztzacuilico   I've come to stop you   *he venido para detenerte*

zan nican   right here   *aquí mismo*
tlantica in monemac   your power ends   *tu poder termina*
ahmo tipanoz   you shall not pass!   *¡no pasarás!*

NEW DAY

NUEVO DÍA

YANCUIC ILHUITL

. . . El chasquido del rayo
abría zanjas de luz
en tus ojos negros y
en la noche
del agua

y en mí nacía la tormenta

. . . Thunder
opened chasms of light
in your dark eyes
in the night
on the water

And in me the storm was born

Lucha Corpi

Heart of the Mountain
Corazón de la montaña
Tepeyollohtli

water's	*el agua*	*ca atl*
the heart of	*es el corazón de*	*iyolloh*
the mountain	*la montaña*	*in tepetl*
its voice:	*su voz:*	*itozqui:*
a jaguar	*un jaguar*	*ocelotl*
of echoes	*de ecos*	*in caquizti*

New Day
Nuevo día
Yancuic ilhuitl

from the hilltop	*desde la cima de la colina*	*tepeticpac*
near my village	*cerca de mi pueblo*	*itloc naltepeuh*
in the distance	*en la distancia*	*huehcapa*
by the cornfields	*en los campos de maíz*	*inahuac milpan*
I saw their glitter	*vi su brillo*	*oniquitta itzontlanca*
their luster	*su lustre*	*ipepetlacaca*
are those giant deer?	*¿serán venados gigantes?*	*cuix hueyi mamazah?*
are they laughing?	*¿están riéndose?*	*cuix huetzcatinemi?*
and I heard	*y oí*	*ihuan oninacazoh*
listened to	*escuché a*	*oniquicac*
the soulbirds:	*los pájaros-alma:*	*in yoltotomeh:*
"trees are crying"	*"los árboles están llorando"*	*"in cuahuitl chochoca"*
a thorn	*una espina*	*ahhuatl*
pierced by tongue	*perforó mi lengua*	*oquicoyonih nonenepil*
and I prayed	*y oré*	*ihuan onitlahtlauhtih*
bleeding	*sangrando*	*inoc nezquizaya*
untied my long	*desaté mi largo*	*oniquehquen*
black hair	*cabello negro*	*notzonquen*
threw to the sky	*eché al cielo*	*in ilhuicac onicontlaz*
my father's bundle	*el bulto de mi padre*	*iquimil notan*
soon night turned	*pronto la noche me volvió*	*in oyohuac*
me into a shadow	*gran sombra*	*oninocuep cehualli*
big enough to cover	*para cubrir*	*in huelitini in*
the whole valley	*todo el valle*	*quitzacua in atlauhtli*
enter and fuel	*para entrar y avivar*	*ma calaquican*
their own campfires	*sus propios campamentos*	*ma tlecuauhtlazcan*
awaiting	*que esperan*	*quichixtoqueh*
the new day!	*al ¡nuevo día!*	*in yancuic ilhuitl!*

Moon
Luna
Metztli

celestial	*gota*	*chichihualoyotl*
drop of milk	*celestial de leche*	*ichipinca in*
of our Mother's	*de los pechos*	*ichichihual Tonantzin*
breast	*de nuestra Madre*	*ilhuicac*

Sun's Children
Los hijos del sol
Ipilhuantzitzin Tonatiuh

although	*aunque*	*in manel*
we may lose	*perdamos*	*tipehualoh*
in battle	*en batalla*	*tlapallan*
we will win	*ganaremos*	*tomahuizzo*
this war	*esta guerra*	*hualahciz*
in peace	*en paz*	*yocoxca*

Night
Noche
Yohualli

how vast	*qúe vasto*	*inic patlahuac*
how enormous	*qué tan enorme*	*inic hueyitepol*
how great	*qué grandioso*	*inic huehcapan*
this empire	*este imperio*	*itlahtohcayo*
of darkness	*de oscuridad*	*in yohuallotl*
and yet	*y así*	*ma tel*
disarmed	*desarmado*	*quitlahuiztoma*
by one	*por una*	*zan ce*
needle	*aguja*	*tonalmitl*
of light	*de luz*	*tlahuilloh*

Flor y canto
Flower and Song
In xochitl in cuicatl

cada árbol	every tree	*cece cuahuitl*
un hermano	a brother	*ca totiachcauh*
cada monte	every hill	*cecen tepetontli*
una pirámide	a pyramid	*ca tzacualli*
un oratorio	a holy spot	*ca teoyocan*
cada valle	every valley	*cecen tepeihtic*
un poema	a poem	*ca cuicayotl*
in xochitl	in xochitl	*in xochitl*
in cuicatl	in cuicatl	*in cuicatl*
flor y canto	flower and song	*xochicuicatl*
cada nube	every cloud	*cecem mixtli*
una plegaria	a prayer	*ca tlahtlauhtiliztli*
cada gota	every rain	*cecen atl*
de lluvia	drop	*ichipinca*
un milagro	a miracle	*ca tlamahuizolli*
cada cuerpo	every body	*cece tlactli*
una orilla	a seashore	*ca atentli*
al mar	a memory	*ca necauhcayotl*
un olvido	at once lost	*poliuhqui*
encontrado	and found	*in oc tlanextilli*
todos juntos—	we all together—	*nehhuantin tocepan—*
luciérnagas	fireflies	*tixoxotlameh*
de la noche	in the night	*yohuatzinco*
soñando	dreaming up	*tictemiquih*
el cosmos	the cosmos	*in cemanahuactli*

Glossary

All words derived from Nahuatl if not otherwise noted.

Acaxochtzin: Reed-Flower, from *acatl*, "reed," *xochitl*, "flower," and the honorific suffix *–tzin*; it is a ritual name for the deer.

Aguamiel: The liquid drawn from the core of the maguey plant before it is fermented and turned into pulque; in Spanish it literally means "honey water."

Antiguos: Spanish for "ancient ones."

Atlinan: Water-Mother, medicinal herb, from *atl*, "water," and *inan*, "it is its mother."

Atole: A thick drink or gruel made of corn mean of various consistencies and flavors; derived from *atolli*, which is formed by *at*, "water," and *tlaolli*, "corn."

Aztec: Nahuatl-speaking group that migrated south from Aztlán, "Place of Herons," which many contemporary Chicanos identify as their U.S. Southwest homeland and which is the origin of the word Aztec; they were also known as the Mexica (pronounced "Meshica"), from which Mexicano and Chicano are derived. In 1325 the Aztecs founded Tenochtitlan on a small island in Lake Texcoco where an eagle was devouring a serpent; they aggressively conquered the surrounding Indian groups and were themselves vanquished by new diseases and a combined Indian-Spanish army led by Hernán Cortés in 1521.

Camotes: Spanish for sweet potatoes, from *camotli*.

Campanilli: Joint-Cracker; in the *Tratado*, the name occurs only in apposition to Xolotl.

Caxxoch: Bowl-Flower, from *caxxochitl*, in turn from *caxitl*, "bowl," and *xochitl*, "flower"; one of the four Tlazolteteo, goddesses of love and filth.

Centeotl: Ear-of-Corn God, from *centli*, "dried ear of corn," and *teotl*, "god"; Ruiz de Alarcón translated it as "the only god," a misinterpretation since he takes here *cen-* to mean "one."

Cenzontle: Derived by apocope from *centzontlatolltototl*, "bird of four hundred songs or voices"; from *centzont-li*, "four hundred," *tlatolli*, "word," and *totl*, "bird"; a tropical songbird appreciated for its great singing versatility.

Chalalatli: A tree with oblong leaves whose root is used to cure the swelling of the head.

Chalchiuhcueye: Jade-Skirt-Owner, from *chalchihuitl*, "jade," *cueitl*, "skirt," and *ye*, "who owns"; goddess of the water.

Chichimec: Term for the nomadic and hunting Indian tribes arriving to Mesoamerica after the Toltecs in the twelfth century; name of the barbaric tribes from the north. Some have identified this word to mean "Dog People." In the *Tratado*, it is also used as a metaphor for a fish hook.

Chicome-Coatl: Seven Snake, from *chicome*, "seven: (*chic-ome*, "five plus two"), and *coatl*, "snake"; a calendric name and goddess of corn; in the *Tratado* it is used as a magical name for corn. It refers to a specific date marking the planting cycle of corn that some have identified as the spring equinox.

Chicome-Xochitl: Seven Flower, from *chicome*, "seven" (*chic-ome*, "five plus two"), and *xochitl* "flower"; a calendrical name; it is a ritual name for the male deer.

Chicomoztoc: Seven-Caves-Place, from *chicome*, "seven" (*chic-ome*, "five plus two"), *oztotl*, "cave," and the suffix *-c*, meaning "place"; this name designates the mythical seven caves from which the Aztecs originated. In the *Tratado* it is used as a metaphor for body cavities.

Chiucnauhtlatecapanilli: Nine-Times-Crushed-One, a metaphorical name for tobacco.

Chiucnauhtlatezohtzontli: Nine-Times-Powdered-One, a metaphorical name for tobacco.

Chiucnauhtlatlamatelolli: Nine-Times-Crumbled-One, a metaphorical name for tobacco.

Cihuacoatl: Woman-Snake, from *cihuatl*, "woman," and *coatl*, "snake"; known as La Llorona in Mexico and the Southwest.

Cipactonal: Alligator-Spirit, from *cipactli*, alligator," and *tonal*, "spirit"; *cipactli* is also the glyph of the first day in the Mesoamerican twenty-day month, symbolizing the first animal able to move from the sea to dry land. Cipactonal is also the first woman in the Mesoamerican primordial couple. In Nahuatl mythology, she is credited (together with her spouse, Oxomoco) with originating the divinatory arts.

Citlalcueye: Star-Skirt-Owner, from *citlalin*, "star," *cueitl*, "skirt," and *ye*, "who owns"; Nahuatl name for the Milky Way.

Coanenepilli: Snake-Tongue, from *coatl*, "snake," and *nenepilli*, "tongue"; medicinal herb against snake bites, among other remedies.

Coatlicue: Snake-Skirted-One, from *coatl*, "snake," and *icue*, "it is her skirt"; fertility goddess.

Codex Borbonicus: Book of Indian pictures and glyphs, probably completed before the arrival of the Europeans in the sixteenth century. The original codex is found in the Palais Bourbon in Paris.

Codex Borgia: Book of Indian pictures and glyphs; the original manuscript is now located in the Biblioteca Nazionale Centrale of Florence; it was once part of the personal library of Antonio da Marco Magliabechi, a Florentine bibliographer and man of letters of the late seventeenth century.

Copal: Tree resin used as incense; *copalli*, "incense."

Corazón: Spanish for "heart."

Cozauhqui: Yellow, this color is usually associated with the east; *cozahuic* is another variant of *cozauhqui*.

Cuate: Term derived from Nahuatl, of common usage in Mexican/Chicano Spanish, meaning "twin," figuratively used for close, intimate friends; from *coatl*, "snake"; two snakes of fire form the exterior ring of the Aztec calendar stone marking the time when Quetzalcoatl meets his double, Xolotl.

Cuaton: Small-Head, from *cuatli*, "head," and the diminutive suffix, *-ton*; one of the four Tlazolteteo, goddesses of love and filth.

Curandera: Spanish for "healer."

Flor: Spanish for "flower."

Guadalupe: Patron saint of Mexico, a syncretic religious figure including Mesoamerican, Christian, and Arabic elements; according to tradition she appeared and spoke in Nahuatl to the Indian Juan Diego in Tepeyac, where Tonantzin, "Our Mother Goddess," was worshipped. She has been linked to several social movements and causes both in Mexico and the Southwest. For example, she was on the first Mexican flag of Father Miguel Hidalgo's Indian army, fighting for independence from Spain in 1810; the banner of the Mestizo popular armies of Emiliano Zapata in the Mexican Revolution of 1910; and also appeared in California on picket signs in the 1965 Delano grape strike, organized by Chicano union leader César Chávez.

Hamaca: Spanish word derived from a Taíno term; "hammock."

Huauhtli: Amaranth; cereal used in molding figurines that were offered and shared as a ritual communion of thanksgiving after the first crop of the year.

Huehueh: Old Man, a metaphor for fire; it is also another name for Oxomoco; in classical times, Huehueteotl, from *huehuetl*, "old man," and *teotl*, "god," was the name of the god of fire, one of the oldest deities in Mesoamerica.

Huipil: A sleeveless cotton tunic used by Indian women as a blouse or dress.

Icnopiltzintli: Orphan-Child, from *icnotl*, "orphan," and *piltzintli*, "child"; this is another name for Centeotl, but it can also be a common noun for "poor orphan."

In ixtli in yollotl: Face and Heart, figurative phrase for truth and sincerity, formed by setting together *ixtli*, "face," and *yollotl*, "heart."

In xochitl in cuicatl: Flower and Song, figurative phrase for poetry, formed by setting together *xochitl*, "flower," and *cuicatl*, "song"; Chicanos have used the Spanish equivalent, floricanto, to name the poetry and cultural festivals in their communities since the late 1960s.

Iztac: White, this color is usually associated with the south.

La Llorona: Spanish for "Crying Woman," a mythical woman who cries up and down looking for her lost children around water sources, very much alive in folk legends throughout Mexico and the Southwest; derived from the Aztec legend of Cihuacoatl, Woman-Snake.

Maguey: Taíno term from the Caribbean region for the plant from which aguamiel (Spanish for "honey water") is drawn and turned into pulque, a fermented alcoholic beverage; its Nahuatl name is *metl*.

Maíz: Spanish word derived from the Taíno name for corn; the Nahuatl equivalent is *taolli*, "dried, shelled corn," or *centli*, "dried, unshelled corn."

Matl: The Hand, in the *Tratado* it is used as another name for Quetzalcoatl.

Mestizo: Spanish word that identifies a person of mixed racial/ethnic background; it no longer carries the negative connotations of its history, nor does it carry the negative connotations of its English equivalents, like "half-breed," "half-caste"; it has been increasingly accepted as a self-identity term by Latinos both in Latin America and the U.S.

Mezquite: A common spiny shrub or small tree in Mexico and the Southwest that produces a medicinal resin; from *mizquitli*, "tree of resin."

Mixcoacihuatl: Mixcoatl's Woman, from Mixcoatl, "Cloud-Snake," and *cihuatl*, "woman"; it is the female deer.

Mixcoatl: Cloud-Snake, from *mixtli*, "cloud," and *coatl*, "snake"; in classical times, Mixcoatl was the god of the hunt.

Mictlan: Land of the Dead, the underworld, which consisted of nine levels, *ChiucnauhMictlan* (from *chiuc-nahui* "five plus four"); by extension, it refers to the supernatural world as a whole.

Moquequeloatzin: The-One-Who-Makes-Fun-of-Himself, another name for Tezcatlipoca.

Moyohualitoatzin.: One-Called-Night, in classical times, this was another manifestation of Xipe Totec, a fertility god.

Nahual: Derived from *nahualli*, "sorcerer" "magician"; in the *Tratado*, it signifies both a sorcerer who supposedly is able to transform himself or herself into an animal and an animal, a tonal, or a guardian spirit that accompanies a person throughout his or her life.

Nahualteuctli: The Enchanter, from *nahualli*, "sorcerer," and *teuctli*, "lord."

Nahuatl: Language from the Uto-Aztecan linguistic family, which historically extended from the Southwest U.S. and Mexico to Central America; spoken by the Toltecs, Aztecs, Pipiles, and many other Indian groups, with hundreds of Spanish and English words deriving from it; the term comes from the verb *nahuati*, "to speak clearly."

Nana: Familiar term for mother; from the endearment *nanatzin*, "little mother."

Nanahuatzin: The Sun, the honorific name of Nanahuatl, "Pustulous One"; Ruiz de Alarcón retells the myth of the creation of the sun in which a sick man afflicted with pustules and sores was the first to throw himself into a fire; flames cleansed him of all disease, and he came out beautiful and shining, converted into the sun.

Nomatca nehuatl: I myself, magical formula for personal empowerment found in most Nahuatl spells in the Tratado; Ruiz de Alarcón translates it as a phrase, "I myself, in person" or "I, in person"; J. Richard Andrews and Ross Hassig translate it as a sentence, with *nehuatl* meaning "I am the one" or "it is I" and *nomatca* as an adverbial modifier, "in person."

Olchipinque: Ones-Dripping-with-Rubber, in the *Tratado*, a metaphor for birds.

Ollin: Movement, the Nahuatl sign for movement can be found at the center of the Sun Stone or Aztec calendar (formed by the glyphs of the four previous eras surrounding the Sun of the present era, *Ollin Tonatiuh*, "The Sun of Movement"); the Nahuatl word for "heart" is derived from it *y-ollotl*, literally, "his mobility," as in *yoliliztli*, "life," the result of transforming motion.

Olmec: Mother culture of the Mesoamerican civilization; it refers to people "from the land of rubber."

Ololiuhqui: Name for a medicinal herb whose seeds are round; from *olo-lihui*, "round like a ball"; it is used as an oracle in the *Tratado*; also known as *coaxiutl*, "snake herb"; it causes hallucinations.

Olpeyauque: Ones-Overflowing-with-Rubber, in the *Tratado*, another metaphor for birds.

Oxomoco: Turpentine-Ointment-Two-Pine-Torches, from *oxitl*, "turpentine ointment," *ome*, "two," and *ocotl*, "pine torches"; *ocote* is a stick of pine kindling. Oxomoco is the first man in the Mesoamerican primordial couple. In Nahuatl mythology, he is credited (together with his spouse, Cipactonal), with originating the divinatory arts. Oxomoco is also known as Huehueh, "Old Man," which, at times, is used as a metaphor for fire.

Petate: Straw mat used for sleeping; from *petatl*, "matting."

Peyote: Name of diverse kinds of cactaceous plants used for medicinal properties; from *peyotl*, "a thing that glimmers, glows"; it is used as the main sacrament of the Native American Church, a Pan-Indian religious/spiritual movement that has extended throughout Native groups in North America.

Piciete: Common tobacco used by peasants, derived from *piztli*, "tiny," and *iyetl*, "tobacco."

Quetzalcoatl: Plumed Serpent, God and cultural hero of a central myth and historic legend in Mexico and Yucatan, where he was known by his Mayan name, Kukulcan. Quetzalcoatl is a compound noun derived from *quetzalli*, "precious feather," and *coatl*, "snake"; he is identified with Ehecatl, the god of wind, and with the planet Venus. In the form of the Toltec cultural hero Ce-Acatl Topiltzin Quetzalcoatl (Ce-Acatl, "One Reed," is his calendrical name, whereas Topiltzin is formed by the prefix *to-*, "our," and *piltzin*, "lord"), he promised to return after being defeated by the priests of the new cult of Tezcatlipoca; Hernán Cortés was identified with this deity when he first appeared on the shores of the Aztec empire in 1519, the year Ce–Atl, which was the date prophesied for the return of Lord Quetzalcoatl.

Siempre: Spanish for "always."

Tehuehuetl: Stone Drum, from *tetl*, "stone," and *huehuetl*, "drum."

Temazcal: Mesoamerican sweat-lodge; derived from *temazcalli*: from *tema*, "to bathe," and *calli*, "house."

Teicxoch: Dream-Flower), compound name from *temictli*, "dream," and *xochitl*, "flower."

Tenexiete: Lime Tobacco), from *tenextli*, "lime" (which is itself a compound noun formed by *tetl*, "stone," and *nextli*, "ash"), and *iyetl*, "tobacco"; it is ground piciete mixed with lime.

Teotihuacan: Place of the Gods), from *teotl*, "god," and *huacan*, "place or surroundings"; one of the most important archeological zones in Mexico, site of the ancient religious and cultural center whose influence extended throughout Mesoamerica; there is evidence that it was sacked and burned around 650 AD.

Tepeyollotli: Heart of the Mountain, from *tepetl*, "mountain," and *yollotli*, "heart"; the jaguar nahual or Tezcatlipoca; also lord of all animals, and responsible for the echo and rumbles of the Earth.

Tezcatlipoca: Smoking Mirror, the god of the sorcerers, also known as Yaotl, "Warrior," and Telpochtli, "The Eternally Young"; originally, he symbolized the night sky, thus his name, "Smoking Mirror," from *tezcatl*, mirror," and *ipoca*, "it emits smoke." A Mesoamerican legend tells how he, jealous of wise Quetzalcoatl, lured the good king into drunkenness and incest with his sister, Xochiquetzal, and then he showed him his face in the "mirror that smokes" and Quetzalcoatl, penitent for his guilt, migrated south and set to sea on a raft of rattlesnakes with the promise that he would return in the year Ce-Acatl ("One Reed"), which was the year Hernán Cortés and his Spanish fleet arrived.

Tlacuilo: Scribe, painter who recorded the hieroglyphs and other symbols in the Nahuatl picture-writing system.

Tlahui: Red Ochre, it is one of the four Tlazolteteo, goddesses of love and filth; this is also the name of Yappan's wife in the myth about the creation of scorpions (see "The Story of Yappan").

Tlaloc: Rain God, from *tlalli*, "land," and *oc*, "one who lies."

Tlamacazqui: Spirit priest, it literally means "one who will give something"; in the *Tratado* it is the term for any power entity.

Tlalteuctli: Ruler of the Earth, from *tlalli*, "land," *teuctli*, "lord"; in the *Tratado*, Ruiz de Alarcón identified this deity as goddess of the earth.

Tlatlauhqui: Red; this color is usually associated with the north; *tlatlahuic* is a variant of *tlatlauhqui*.

Tlazoteotl: Love Goddess, from *tlazotli*, "beloved," and *teotl*, "god, goddess"; the plural form is *Tlazolteteo*, "Love Goddesses."

Tlazolteteo: Love Goddesses, from *tlazotli*, beloved," and *teteo*, "gods, goddesses," the plural of *teotl*, "god, goddess"; in the *Tratado* there are four deities associated with the goddesses of love and filth: Cuaton, Caxxoch, Tlahui, Xapel.

Tlazopilli: Beloved Prince, Beloved Princess, a ritual name for corn; from *tlazotli*, "precious, beloved thing," and *pilli*, "nobleman, noblewoman."

Toltec: Nahuatl-speaking Indian group whose capital was Tollan; for later Indians in Mesoamerica, *toltecatl* signified "artist."

Tonacacihuatl: Lady of Our Flesh, from the prefix *to-*, "our," *nactli*, "flesh," "sustenance," and *cihuatl*, "woman"; another name for *Xochiquetzal*, it is also used in the *Tratado* as a ritual name for corn.

Tonal: Soul, spirit, from the Nahuatl word *tonalli*, "sun like," which is derived from the verb *tona*, "to shine, to be sunny, to be warm."

Tonalamatl: Book or codex of days or destinies, a compound name formed by *tonal*, "day," "destiny," "spirit," and *amatl*, "bark paper"; it was a book used for divination and as an astrological almanac.

Tonantzin: Our Mother, from the prefix *to-*, "our," and *nantli*, "mother," together with the suffix *-tzin*, which indicates endearment and respect; Nahuatl name for the Virgen de Guadalupe, the patron saint of Mexico; in classical times, it was another name for Centeotl, the corn deity.

Tonatiuh: Sun God, the name of the Fifth Sun in the Nahuatl creation myth.

Topan: The Heaven, celestial realm, also called *ChiucnauhTopan* (from *chiuc-nahui*, "five plus four") because it had nine levels.

Verde: Spanish for "green."

Xapel: Name of one of the four goddesses of love and filth (Tlazolteteo).

Xochipilli: Flower-Lord, from *xochitl*, "flower," and *pilli*, "nobleman"; patron of festivities and poetry and symbol of summer.

Xochiquetzal: Flower-Plume, love goddess; from *xochitl*, "flower," and *quetzalli*, "precious plume"; goddess of flowers, arts, and crafts. Also known as Tonacacihuatl and Chalchiuhtlicue.

Xochitl: Flower, also the last day of the Mesoamerican twenty-day month.

Xolotl: The Double, name of Quetzalcoatl's double; he is a god who appears in the *Tratado* in apposition to Capanilli.

Xoxouhqui: Green, this color is usually associated with the west; *xoxohuic* is a variant of *xoxouhqui*.

Yaotl: The Warrior, another name for Tezcatlipoca.

Yappan: Black-Corn-Flag, metaphorical name for the black scorpion.

Yauhtli: Sweet marigold or anise, a medicinal herb used for incense; from *iyauhtli*, "offering flower," and *iyahua*, "smoke offering."

Yayauhqui: Dusky, dark in color; *yayahuic* is a variant of *yayauhqui*.

Yoliliztli: Life in Motion, from *yollotl*, "heart," which itself derives as *y-ollotl*, "his movement," from *ollin*, "movement," the principle of life.

Yolloxochitl: Magnolia, from *yollotl*, "heart," and *xochitl*, "flower."

Yohuallahuantzin: Night-Drinker, another name for Xipe Totec, a fertility god, in classic times.

Bibliography

Aguirre Beltran, Gonzalo. *Medicina y magia: El proceso de aculturación en la estructura colonial*. Mexico City: Instituto Nacional Indigenista, Colección de Antropología Social, no. 1, 1963.

Andrews, J. Richard. *Introduction to Classical Nahuatl*. Austin: University of Texas Press, 1975.

Andrews, J. Richard, and Ross Hassig, eds. and trans. *Treatise on the Heathen Superstitions That Today Live Among the Indians Native to This New Spain, 1692*, by Hernando Ruiz de Alarcón. Norman: University of Oklahoma Press, 1984.

Beck, Peggy V., Anna Lee Walters and Nia Francisco. *The Sacred: Ways of Knowledge, Sources of Life*. Flagstaff, Ariz.: Navajo Community College Press and Northland Publishing Co., 1990.

Bierhorst, John. *A Nahuatl–English Dictionary and Concordance to the "Cantares Mexicanos," with an Analytic Transcription and Grammatical Notes*. Stanford, Calif.: Stanford University Press, 1985.

Bierhorst, John. *Cantares Mexicanos: Songs of the Aztecs*. Stanford, Calif.: Stanford University Press, 1985.

Bierhorst, John. *Four Masterworks of American Indian Literature: Quetzalcoatl, the Ritual of Condolence, Cuceb, the Night Chant*. New York: Farrar, Straus and Giroux, 1974.

Bierhorst, John. *"On the Nature of Aztec Poetry,"* Review 29: 69–71. New York: Inter-American Relations, 1981.

Bierhorst, John. *The Sacred Path: Spells, Prayers and Power Songs of the American Indian*. New York: Quille, 1983.

Brinyon, Daniel G. *Ancient Nahuatl Poetry*. New York: AMS Press, 1969.

Cabrera, Luis. *Diccionario de aztequismos*. Mexico City: Oasis, 1980.

Cardenal, Ernesto. *Quetzalcoatl*. Translated by Clifton Ross. Berkeley, Calif.: New Earth Publications, 1990.

Carrasco, David. *Quetzalcoatl and the Irony of Empire*. Chicago: University of Chicago Press, 1982.

Caso, Alfonso. *Los calendarios prehispánicos*. Mexico City: Universidad Nacional Autónoma de México, Instituto de Investigaciones Históricas, 1967.

Coe, Michael D. and Gordon Whittaker, eds and trans. *Aztec Sorcerers in Seventeenth Century Mexico: The Treatise on Superstitions by Hernando Ruiz de Alarcón*. Albany: State University of New York at Albany, Institute for Mesoamerican Studies, no. 7. 1982.

Corpi, Lucha. *Variaciones sobre una tempestad / Variations on a Storm*. Berkeley, Calif.: Third Woman Press, 1990.

de Gerez, Toni. *2-Rabbit, 7-Wind: Poems from Ancient Mexico Retold from Nahuatl Texts*. New York: Viking, 1971.

Fellows, W. H. *"The Treatises of Hernando Ruiz de Alarcón."* Tlalocan, vol. 7: 309–55. Mexico City: Universidad Nacional Autónoma de México, Instituto de Investigaciones Históricas, 1977.

Field, Frederick V. *Pre-Hispanic Mexican Stamp Designs*. New York: Dover Publications, 1974.

Garibay K., Angel María. *Historia de la literatura náhuatl*, 2 vols. Mexico City: Editorial Porrúa, 1953–54.

González, Rafael J. "Symbol and Metaphor in Nahuatl Poetry," *ETC.: A Review of General Semantics*, 25, no. 4, 1968.

Guerra, Fray Juan. *Arte de la lengua mexicana que fue usual entre los indios del obispado de Guadalajara y parte de los de Durango y Michoacán, escrito en 1692 por Fr. Juan Guerra, predicador y definidor de la Provincia Franciscanos de Santiago de Jalisco*. 2nd ed. by Alberto Santoscoy. Guadalajara, Mexico: Imprenta Ancira y Hermano. A. Ochoa, 1990.

Hinz, Eike. *Anthropologische Analyse altaztekischer Texte, Teil 1: Die magischen Texte im Tratado Ruiz de Alarcons*. Hamburg: Kommisionverl. Kalus Renner, 1970.

Horcasitas, Fernando. *The Aztecs Then and Now. Mexico City*: Minutiae Mexicana, 1974.

Karttunen, Frances. *An Analytical Dictionary of Nahuatl*. Austin: University of Texas Press, 1983.

Kissam, Edward. "Aztec Poems," *Antaeus* (New York), no. 4 (Winter 1971): 7–17.

Kissam, Edward, and Michael Schmidt. *Flower and Song: Poems of the Aztec Peoples*. London: Anvil Press Poetry, 1977.

LaFaye, Jacques. *Quetzalcoatl and Guadalupe: The Formation of Mexican National Consciousness*, 1531–1813, trans. Benjamin Keen. Chicago: University of Chicago Press, 1976.

Leander, Brigitta. *In xochitl in cuicatl / Flor y canto: La poesía de los aztecas*. Mexico City: Instituto Nacional Indigenista, 1972.

Leander, Brigitta. *Native Mesoamerican Spirituality: Ancient Myths, Discourses, Stories, Doctrines, Hymns, Poems from the Aztec, Yucatec, Quiche-Maya and other Sacred Traditions*. New York: Paulist Press, 1980.

Leander, Brigitta. *Pre-Columbian Literatures of Mexico*. Norman: University of Oklahoma Press, 1968.

López Austin, Alfredo. "Conjuros médicos de los nahuas," *Revista de la Universidad de México*, 24, no. 11, i–xvi, 1970.

López Austin, Alfredo. "Conjuros nahuas del siglo XVII," *Revista de la Universidad de México*, 27, no. 4, i–xvi, 1972.

López Austin, Alfredo. "Cuarenta clases de magos del mundo náhuatl," *Estudios de Cultura Náhuatl*, vol. 7: 87 – 117, 1968.

López Austin, Alfredo. "Términos del nahuallatolli," *Historia Mexicana*, 17, no. 1, 1967: 1–36.

López Austin, Alfredo. "Textos de medicina náhuatl." Mexico City: Universidad Nacional Autónoma de México, Instituto de Investigaciones Históricas, 1975.

Macazaga Ordoño, César. *Diccionario de la lengua náhuatl*. Mexico City: Editorial Innovación, 1979.

Mönnich, Anneliese. "*La supervivencia de antiguas representaciones indígenas en la religión popular de los nawas de Veracruz y Puebla.*" In Luis Reyes García and Dieter Christensen, eds., *Der Ring aus Tlalocan: Mythen und Gebete, Lider und Erzählungen der heutigen Nahhua in Veracruz and Pueblo, Mexico / El Anillo de Tlalocan: Mitos, oraciones, cantos y cuentos de los nawas actuales en los estados de Veracruz y Puebla, México*. Berlin: Gebr. Mann Verlag, 1976: 139–44.

Nicholson, Irene. *Firefly in the Night: A Study of Ancient Mexican Poetry and Symbolism*. London: Faber and Faber, 1959.

Paso y Troncoso, Francisco del. *La botánica entre los nahuas y otros estudios*. Pilar Márquez, ed. Mexico City: Secretaría de Educación Pública, 1988.

Ponce, Pedro. "Breve relación de los dioses y ritos de la gentilidad," *Anales del Museo Nacional de México*, vol. 6, 1892: 3–11.

Ponce, Pedro. "Brief Relation of the Gods and Rites of Heathenism." In J. Richard Andrews and Ross Hassig, eds. and trans., *Treatise on the Heathen Superstitions That Today Live Among the Indians Native to This New Spain, 1629, by Hernando Ruiz de Alarcón*. Norman: University of Oklahoma Press, 1984: 211–18.

Quezada, Noemí. *Amor y magia amorosa entre los aztecas: Supervivencia en el México colonial*. Mexico City: Universidad Nacional Autónoma de México, Instituto de Investigaciones Antropológicas, 1975.

Ruiz de Alarcón, Hernando. *Aztec Sorcerers in Seventeenth Century Mexico: The Treatise on Superstitions by Hernando Ruiz de Alarcón*. Michael D. Coe and Gordon Whittaker, eds. and trans. Albany: State University of New York at Albany, Institute for Mesoamerican Studies, publication no. 7, 1982.

Ruiz de Alarcón, Hernando, ed. Francisco del Paso y Troncoso. "Tratado de las supersticiones y costumbres gentílicas que hoy viven entre los indios naturales desta Nueva España," *Anales del Museo Nacional de México*, vol. 6, 1892: 125–223.

Ruiz de Alarcón, Hernando, ed. Francisco del Paso y Troncoso. "Tratado de las supersticiones y costumbres gentílicas que hoy viven entre los indios naturales desta Nueva España," In Jacinto de la Serna et al., notes and introduction by Francisco de Paso y Troncoso, *Tratado de las idolatrías, supersticiones, dioses, ritos, hechicerías y otras costumbres gentílicas de las razas aborígenes de México*, 2 vols. Mexico City: Navarro, Ediciones Fuente Cultural, 1953–54, vol. 2: 17–180.

Ruiz de Alarcón, Hernando. "Tratado de las supersticiones y costumbres gentílicas que hoy viven entre los indios naturales desta Nueva España," In Pedro Ponce, Pedro Sánchez de Aguilar, et al. *El alma encantada: Anales del Museo Nacional de México. Presentación de Fernando Benítez*. Mexico City: Instituto Nacional Indigenista / Fondo de Cultura Económica, 1987: 123–224. (Facsimile edition of Anales del Museo Nacional de México, vol. 6, 1892).

Ruiz de Alarcón, Hernando. *Treatise on the Heathen Superstitions That Today Live Among the Indians Native to This New Spain, 1692, by Hernando Ruiz de Alarcón*. J. Richard and Ross Hassig, eds. and trans. Norman: University of Oklahoma Press, 1984.

Sandoval, Rafael. *Arte de la lengua mexicana: Prólogo y notas de Alfredo López Austin*. Mexico City: Universidad Autónoma Nacional de México, Instituto de Investigaciones Históricas, 1965.

Sawyer-Lauçanne, Christopher. *The Destruction of the Jaguar: Poems from the Books of Chilam Balam*. San Francisco: City Lights Books, 1987.

Séjourné, Laurette. *Burning Water: Thought and Religion in Ancient Mexico*. London: Thames and Hudson, 1957.

Séjourné, Laurette. *El pensamiento náhuatl cifrado por los calendarios*. Mexico City: Siglo XXI, 1981.

Séjourné, Laurette. *El universo de Quetzalcóatl*. Mexico City: Fondo de Cultura Económica, 1962.

Serna, Jacinto de la. "Manual de ministros de indios para el conocimiento de sus idolatrías, y extirpación de ellas," *Anales del Museo Nacional de México*, vol. 6, 1892: 261–480.

Siméon, Rémi. *Diccionario de la lengua náhuatl o mexicana*. Translated by Josefina Oliva de Coll. Mexico City: Siglo XXI, 1977.

Siméon, Rémi. *Dictionnaire de la lengue náhuatl ou mexicaine*. Graz, Austria: Akademische Druck and Verlagsanstalt, 1963. Reprint of the 1885 ed.

Spence, Lewis. *Arcane Secrets and Occult Lore of Mexico and Mayan Central America*. London: Rider and Co., 1930.

Villanueva, Tino. *Crónica de mis años peores*. La Jolla, Calif.: Lalo Press, 1987.

Wasson, R. Gordon, et al. *María Sabina and Her Mazatec Mushroom Velada*. New York: Harcourt Brace Jovanovich, 1974.

Waters, Frank. *Mexico Mystique: The Coming Sixth World of Consciousness*. Chicago: The Swallow Press, 1989.

Translation Credits

The following poems were translated both into Nahuatl by David Bowles and Spanish by Xánath Caraza:

"Silence / El silencio / In cactimaniliztli"

"Same / Lo mismo / Tinehneuhqueh"

"To Those Who Have Lost Everything / Para aquellos que han perdido todo / Itechpa in
   aquihqueh oquipolohcah mocheh"

"Heart / Corazón / Teyolloh"

"Dream-Flower / Flor-de-sueños / Temicxoch"

"I Myself / Yo mismo / Nonohmatcah nehhuatl"

"Midnight Water Song / Canción del agua de la medianoche / Yohualnepantlah acuicatl"

"Martín de Luna"

"Day and Night / Día y noche / Tlahcah yohualtica"

"Heart-Flower / Corazón-Flor / Yolloxochitl"

"Wisdom Seeds / Semillas de sabiduría / Ololiuhqui"

"Cutting Wood / Cortar leña / Nicuauhtzahtzayana"

"Birds / Pájaros / Totomeh"

"Little Toltecs / Toltequitas / Toltecatotontin"

"First Offering / Primera ofrenda / In achtopa huentli"

"Honeywater / Aguamiel / Necuatl"

"Clouds / Nubes / Mixitl"

"Urban Villagers / Aldeanos urbanos / Altepetlacah"

"Potent Seeds / Semillas potentes / Achtli huelitic"

"Home Spirit / Espíritu de casa / In calli iyollo"

"For Love / Para el amor / Ipampa in notlazohtlaliz"

"Nature / Naturaleza / In yoliliztli"

"Tobacco / Tabaco / Piciyetl"

"Soul / Alma / Motonal"

"Wiser / Sabio / Nihmati"

"Birth / Nacimiento / Tlacatiliztli"

"Reconciling / Reconciliación / Netetlazohtlaltilo"

"Face and Heart / Cara y corazón / In ixtli in yollotl"

"Domingo Hernández"

"Herbs / Hierbas / In pahtli"

"Snake Woman / La Llorona / Cihuacoatl"

"Massage / Masaje / Nepahpacholiztli"

"Holocaust / Holocausto / Mixtlatihtoqueh"

"Working Hands / Manos trabajadoras / Noma tlaayini"

"Not Poems / No poemas / Ahmo xochicuicatl"

"Heart of the Mountain / Corazón de la montaña / Tepeyollohtli"

"New Day / Nuevo día / Yancuic ilhuitl"

"Moon / Luna / Metztli"

"Sun's Children / Los hijos del sol / Ipilhuantzitzin Tonatiuh"

"Night / Noche / Yohualli"

The following poems were translated into Nahuatl by David Bowles:

"Four Directions / Cuatro direcciones / Nauhcampa"
"In the Middle of the Night / En medio de la noche / Ticatla"
"I'm Not Really Crying / En verdad no estoy llorando / Ahmo huel nichoca"
"Shame / Vergüenza / Nopinahuiz"
"Mestizo / Mestizo / Otomitl"
"Matriarch / Matriarca / Cihuatlahtoani"
"Rescue / Rescate / Maquixtilo"
"Spirit Book / Libro de espíritus / Tonalamatl"
"Spirit Animal / Nahual / Nonahual"
"Movement / Movimiento / Ollin"
"Never Alone / Nunca solos / Ayic toceltin"
"Morning Ritual / Ritual matutino / Notequitzin in yohuantzinco"
"Seven Flower / Siete Flor / Chicome-Xochitl"
"Spirits of the Forest / Espíritus del bosque / Cuauhtlah tlamacazqueh"
"Seven Snake / Siete Serpiente / Chicome-Coatl"
"Calendar Keepers / Guardianes del calendario / Tonalpouhqueh"
"Thunder / Trueno / Cuacualachtli"
"Rainbow / Arcoíris / Ayauh cozamalotl"
"Water Spirits / Espíritus de agua / Tlamacazqueh in atl"
"Song for Tortillas / Canto a las tortillas / Tlaxcalcuicatl"
"Ode to Tomatoes / Oda a los jitomates / Xitomacuicatl"
"Drought / Sequía / Huaccayotl"
"Seer / Visionario / Ontlachiyani"
"Visions / Visiones / Tlachiyaliztli"
"Listen / Escucha / Xitlacaquican"
"Oracle / Oráculo / Achtopaihtoani"
"Life in Motion / Vida en moción / Yoliliztli"
"Messengers / Mensajeros / Titlantin"
"Flowers / Flores / Xochimeh"
"We're one / Somos uno / Tichentlacah"
"Hernando Ruiz de Alarcón (1587–1646)"
"Snake Wheel / Rueda víbora / Temalacacoatl"
"Mother / Madre / Tonantzin"
"Flower and Song / Flor y canto / In xochitl in cuicatl"

The following poems were translated into Spanish by Xánath Caraza:

"Journey"
"Nehnemi itlahtlauhtiliz / Traveler's Prayer / Oración del viajero"
"Tonatiuh itlahtlauhtiliz in ayamo nemohua / Prayer for the Sun Before Traveling / Oración para el sol antes de viajar"
"Inic amihua in totomeh / For Hunting Birds / Para cazar pájaros"
"Inic amihua in mamazah / For Hunting Deer / Para cazar venado"
"Mazatl tlatzonhauzhuilli / Ensnared Deer / Venado atrapado"
"Inic in yolcatl totoco milpan / For Keeping Animals Our of Sown Fields / Para mantener los animales fuera de los campos sembrados"

"Inhuicpa in azcameh ahcemeleh / Against Unruly Ants / Contra hormigas revoltosas"
"Intechpa in tlalocuiltin in ayamo michmalo / To Earthworms Before Fishing with a Hook /
A los gusanos de tierra antes de pescar con un gancho"
"Inic aquilo in cintli / For Planting Corn / Para sembrar maíz"
"Inic motlatia in cintli / For Storing Corn / Para almacenar maíz"
"Inic aquilo in camohtli / For Planting Camotes / Para sembrar camotes"
"Ihuicpa in tecualan / Against Anger / Contra el enojo"
"Inic tecochtlazalo / To Cast Sleep / Para conjurar el sueño"
"Inic quixinilo in cochtlazaliztli / To Undo the Sleep Spell / Para deshacer el conjuro del
sueño"
"Inic namico tetlazohtlaliz / For Finding Affection / Para encontrar afecto"
"Inic maltia / For Bathing / Para bañarse"
"Achtopaihtolo matica / Divining with the Hands / Adivinar con las manos"
"Itlahtlauhtiliz in tletl / Prayer to Fire / Oración al fuego"
"Achtopaihtolo ica centli / Divining with Corn / Adivinar con maíz"
"Tlaachtopaihtoliztli ittalli in atl / Divining by Looking in the Water / Adivinación mirando
en el agua"
"Ipampa telpan cococ / For Strained Chests / Para los pechos cansados"
"Ipampa nepoztequiliztli / For Bone Fractures / Para fracturas de hueso"
"Tetzotzopitzaliztli ipampa in tetepotz / Acupuncture for the Back / Acupuntura para la
espalda"
"Ihuicpa in totonqui / For Fevers / Para la fiebre"
"Ihuicpa in ciyahuiztli auh in coacihuiztli / For Fatigue and Body Pains / Para la fatiga y
los dolores de cuerpo"
"Itlaquetzal Yappan / The Story of Yappan / El cuento de Yappan"
"Ihuicpa itlaminal ihuan iztlac in colotl / Against Scorpion's Sting and Poison / Contra la
picadura y veneno del escorpión"

About the Author

FRANCISCO X. ALARCÓN was a Chicano poet and educator. The author of thirteen volumes of poetry and seven children's books, he was the recipient of literary prizes including the Before Columbus Foundation's American Book Award, the PEN Oakland/ Josephine Miles Award, and the University of California, Irvine, Chicano/Latino Literary Prize. He taught at the University of California, Davis, where he directed the Spanish for Native Speakers Program.

About the Editor

ODILIA GALVÁN RODRÍGUEZ is a poet, writer, editor, and activist. She is the author of six volumes of poetry. Her latest, *The Color of Light*, (FlowerSong Books, 2019) is an extensive collection of chronicles and poetry honoring the Mexica (Aztec) and Orisha (Yorùbá) Energies, which she worked on during her time living in Cuba and Mexico. Also, along with the late Francisco X. Alarcón, she edited the award-winning anthology *Poetry of Resistance: Voices for Social Justice* (University of Arizona Press, 2016). Galván Rodríguez has worked as an editor for various print media such as *Matrix Women's News Magazine*, *Community Mural's Magazine*, and *Tricontinental Magazine* in Havana, Cuba. She is currently the editor of *Cloud Women's Quarterly Journal* online and facilitates creative writing workshops nationally. As an activist she worked for the United Farm Workers of America, AFL-CIO and the East Bay Institute for Urban Arts, has served on numerous boards and commissions, and is currently active in women's organizations whose mission it is to educate around environmental justice issues and disseminate an indigenous worldview regarding the earth and people's custodial relationship to it.